Cleveland
in Early Postcards
1900-1930

by *Ralph Burnham Thompson*

Introduction by Walter Leedy

The Vestal Press, Ltd.
Vestal, NY

Cover design by Don Bell

The Cleveland title on the cover is adapted from the logo found on many early Cleveland postcards published by Braun Art Publishing Company, established in Cleveland in 1904 by Oscar Braun. The company expanded from the Braun home into the garage, eventually outgrowing those premises. In 1955, the successor, now named Charmcraft, merged with Arcadia Greeting Card Company of Detroit, and the name was changed to United States Greeting Card Company. Those headquarters were located at 1962 E. 57th Street in Cleveland from around 1955 to about 1965 when we lose track of the company. No record of the trademark's being registered could be found at the time of this book's publication. The publisher appreciates the help of staff members of the Cleveland Public Library for information regarding the Braun Art Publishing Company.

The Mountcastle map on the inside front cover dates from around 1939, published by the Mountcastle Map Company which was located at 1435 East 12th Street in Cleveland. Unfortunately, no further information on this company could be found.

Thompson, Ralph Burnham
    Cleveland in picture postcards, 1900-1930 / by Ralph Burnham Thompson.
        p.   cm.
    Includes bibliographical references.
    ISBN 0-911572-90-2 (pbk. : A-free) : $11.95
    1. Cleveland (Ohio)--Pictorial works. 2. Postcards--Ohio--Cleveland. I. Title.
    F499. C643T46 1992
    977.1'32041'0222--dc20   92-15449
                                             CIP

Printed in the United States of America
First printing October 1992

99 98 97 96 95 94 93 92   10 9 8 7 6 5 4 3 2 1

Table of Contents

Foreword

Originally, when the idea for this book was discussed, Russell Hehr was our logical choice — he had already co-authored *Euclid Beach Park Is Closed for the Season*, and *Euclid Beach Park, A Second Look*, and had written and lectured on architecture, art history, amusement parks, roller coasters, Santa Claus, Christmas, and creches. He was assistant head of Fine Arts and Special Collections at the Cleveland Public Library, and a collector of picture postcards of Cleveland. He had begun work on this book, accumulating postcards and writing descriptions, when he died.

Fortunately, Ralph Thompson came to the rescue. A postcard collector who is particularly interested in railroads, he was an experienced researcher and published writer, and he was a Cleveland enthusiast with many happy memories of the early days in his home town. Actually, Mr. Thompson was not born in Cleveland — his parents arrived six months too late for that to happen. His father came to serve as pastor of the Glenville Church (see page 73) in October, 1912. A photograph taken in May, 1914, shows our author pointing, and the caption in the photo album reads, "Ding ding car!" Thus we see Mr. Thompson's early interest in pointing out the scenery, particularly trolleys. As you read his descriptions accompanying the postcards, you will note that his interest in trolleys is still very strong.

Karl Owen Thompson, our author's father, began teaching English at Case School of Applied Science in 1914, a temporary job which lasted until 1947. He did not succumb to the lure of the motor car until 1925, so until that time he used the street car to get around for both business and pleasure. A "trolley buff," he took our author and his brother Paul on trips to explore different lines around the city. When the family moved to the Rosedale School area between Wade Park and Superior Avenues, they used those two lines. Between 1915 and 1925, numerous trips were taken on the Cleveland Railway Company and the Cleveland, Painesville and Eastern (interurban) Railway when the elder Mr. Thompson assisted at the Congregational Church in "Euclid Village." They rode on old wooden cars, dinkeys, "new" steel cars (1100 series), and big red interurbans.

The family moved to Cleveland Heights and Ralph attended Roxboro Junior High and Heights High. He thus became familiar with the Cedar Road and Fairmount Boulevard trolley and the Lee Road bus. In fact, the Thompsons were among the first riders when the bus began to operate in 1925. (The Cleveland Railway Company was said to be the first large streetcar system to add buses, having decided in 1925 that the motor vehicle was here to stay.) Electric traction almost disappeared from Cleveland's streets by 1954.

After going off to college at Antioch and Miami, Ralph Thompson returned to Cleveland and began to work on the west side and downtown. He later left Cleveland for academia in Texas and Florida, but kept up with changes in both the landscape and the transit system of Cleveland by frequent visits and the works of Harry Christiansen and Kenneth S. P. Morse. This continuing interest in his home town, plus Russell Hehr's notes which, Mr. Thompson says, were very inspiring, have provided the basis for this book.

Introduction

Cleveland, Ohio, is a city that had only been founded in 1796. Growing from a population of 57 in 1810 to 260,000 in 1890, Cleveland emerged from its pioneer, log-cabin days to become a major industrial center of 381,000 by 1900, which made it the seventh largest city in the United States. By 1930 the industrial metropolis had soared to nearly one million people.

After the Civil War, sweeping technological changes fundamentally altered the lives of many Clevelanders and challenged the very structure of American society. A national railroad system, coupled with telegraph and eventually telephone networks, revolutionized communications. With new means of production, extraction of mineral resources, techniques of preserving food, and mechanized agriculture, basic industries began to specialize and multiply to create a national market. The concepts of the national corporation and national advertising were born.

By the end of the nineteenth century, Cleveland emerged as a research as well as a manufacturing center, because local conditions fostered an atmosphere of experimentation. Cleveland was the first city in the world to have its streets extensively lighted by electricity and the first place in the United States to make a commercial success of the Bessemer process for refining steel; and it was home to several pioneer firms in the American mixed paint and varnish industry. Cleveland's leaders, however, were financially conservative. Although there were no bank failures and comparatively few business failures during the recession from 1893 to 1896, the working class was poor, and unemployment was high. Nevertheleses attracted by the chance of industrial employment, immigrants flooded into the community (almost 125,000 were foreign born in 1900) making Cleveland a hodgepodge of ethnic enclaves.

These profound transformations, however, carried the promise of increased wealth for the nation and, indeed, as general wealth increased, Cleveland's middle class grew in size. As a consequence, leisure time increased. These circumstances made recreational travel a real possibility for more people.

Entrepreneurial American businessmen recognized the opportunity to create a new need: stimulated by travel to the World's Columbian Exposition of 1893, the postcard era was born and popularized, reaching its zenith before World War II. Other factors too were responsible for the debut of the picture postcard. Important amongst them were the invention of photography, reasonably priced and abundant card stock, inexpensive inks and mechanical presses that could literally print thousands of postcards per hour, not to mention cheap postal rates. These factors made postcards accessible to the general population. Consequently, the depicted subjects, as well as the cards' *raison d'être*, reflected popular sentiments and current societal values and aspirations.

It was through the picture postcard that individuals communicated the quick, short message which oft times carried the bragging "wish you were here" missive. They also served as "mail memories" in an era when photography was just becoming available to the general population. Most important, they were promulgated by community leaders to communicate instantaneously the wealth and cultural resources of their cities: every civic booster came to realize that a good picture was worth a thousand words. Thus the postcard was a most powerful form of national advertising in an emerging era of mass media and communications.

Picture postcards had other functions as well. For example, realizing that the ordinary Clevelander might rally behind a rendering of a proposed new railway station to be located adjacent to the Public Square, the developers behind the project—the Van Sweringen interests—conducted an illustrated-postcard campaign to bridge the gap between the architect's conception and the layman's appreciation with the intent to influence the public referendum of 6 January 1919: the Public Square site for a new union station was approved by the citizens of Cleveland by a vote of 30,731 to 19,859. As a result of the efficacy of this postcard campaign, Cleveland's physical form was fundamentally altered: the Terminal Tower was built. Completed in 1930, this 708-foot high skyscraper instantly became Cleveland's centerpiece, her most recognizable marker and an enduring symbol for community pride. Interestingly, when the Union Terminal Station located below the Terminal Tower was recently transformed into a downtown shopping mall—called "The Avenue"—this reuse project was successfully brought to the attention of potential national and international tenants who were not already in the Cleveland market by a direct-mail postcard campaign. Therefore, even today the postcard still plays a role as a business stratagem.

Furthermore, capitalizing on the commercial potential of the inherently popular appeal that postcards engendered, publishers created a new need by printing sets of postcards specifically to be collected and placed in albums rather than actually being mailed. For this purpose numbers were placed on the face of cards, such as many of those published for the Great Lakes Exposition. Held in 1936-37, this exposition provided the populous with relief from the Depression and offered Clevelanders the opportunity to celebrate the centennial of the incorporation of Cleveland as a city and to make a bragging, assertive statement about the strengths of the Great Lakes region. Therefore, postcard companies themselves developed and promoted the postcard as a collectible.

The subjects depicted on the postcards of Cleveland almost always reflect and support the illusion of a most positive— almost utopian—environment rather than the actual reality of everyday urban life. The depiction of slums, the houses of the working people, and natural disasters such as fires, etc., are an insignificant percentage of subjects depicted on the literally thousands of different postcards that have been published of Cleveland scenes.

Yet, in a few instances postcards have served Clevelanders as powerful, visual, commemorative vehicles as well as satisfying a certain aspect of the public's curiosity for the macabre, such as a 1908 fire at Lakeview Elementary School in the village of Collinwood—now part of Cleveland—in which 172 students and two teachers lost their lives. Postcards of the fire-damaged school surely influenced public opinion and played a role in calling for more thorough school building inspections across the country as well as in Cleveland.

Taken as a whole, postcards of Cleveland scenes, however, communicate the texture of a vigorous and strong— even if partly fictive—environment in which to live. They depict the full gamut of elements which transformed Cleveland from a pioneer village into a sustained and urbane metropolitan environment, such as parks, recreational and pleasure facilities, bridges and transport systems, houses and apartment houses, sacred structures, schools, libraries and cultural institutions, establishments which support ethnic pride and heritage, public commemorative and didactic sculpture, business and industry, and environments designed for shopping.

The postcards of Cleveland, therefore, reflect her collective image and the optimism that pervaded society during the period 1900 to the beginning of World War II. Today these picture postcards enable us to visualize the past— many of the buildings and environmental assemblages have now vanished. Furthermore, postcards hold the potential to teach us the values which have influenced the built environment of Cleveland, thereby helping us to inform the future. They are, also, just fun to look at and collect.

Walter Leedy
Cleveland State University

Public Square

Moses Cleveland Monument Cleveland, O.

Cleveland, Ohio, was founded by Moses Cleaveland of Canterbury, Connecticut, and named in his honor by his surveyors in 1796. The "a" in his name was retained by the surveyors but soon dropped, it is said, by the editor of an early newspaper to save space. That move has saved a lot of space and ink in the past two centuries.

During his lifetime, 1754-1806, Moses Cleaveland served in the Revolutionary War as an officer under General Washington at Valley Forge. A graduate of Yale University, he practiced law in his hometown after the war. He became a founder of the Connecticut Land Company and, in 1796, was sent as the company's agent to survey its holdings along the shore of Lake Erie. This land was part of the Western Reserve of the State of Connecticut. The Cleaveland party sailed along the south shore of Lake Erie from Buffalo through what was then unchartered territory. They entered the Cuyahoga River and landed on its east bank at a point probably near the foot of present-day St. Clair Avenue.

Cleaveland's statue, dedicated in 1880, is located in Public Square.

The New Englanders who laid out Cleveland reserved a five-acre site at a high point south of Lake Erie and east of the Cuyahoga River for a Commons or Public Square. Even as late as 1912 when this photo facing west was taken, it retained a somewhat small-town flavor. Men are lounging on park benches or strolling toward the single trolley. In the center at a distance, the Rockefeller Building can be seen. The tall structure facing the Square is the Ulmer Building, later known as the Public Square Building

The photographer for this scene is standing in the center of the four quadrants of Public Square facing south. Note the cobblestone streets. Cars of the Cleveland Electric Railway were of a different color for each line. If the colors are true, the approaching car is blue and has come north from Woodland Avenue on Ontario Street. The car on the opposite line is yellow and will be going to Wade Park via Prospect Avenue. May's Drug Store stood for many years on the southwest corner while May's Department Store (no relation) stood on the east side on Ontario Street.

Today, we wonder how such a bridge and waterway had room to exist in the southwest quadrant of the square. Note the newsboys with their caps, typical of those worn by boys until the 1930s; long jackets; tight-fitting knickers buttoned above the knee; long black stockings; and high, buttoned shoes.

Bridge in Public Square.

This scene represents trolley riding near its peak in 1920. A number of electric railway lines were built to other cities: Painesville, Akron, Canton, Mansfield, Toledo, and Detroit. The station was in one of the old buildings on the right; an Akron interurban is loading in front of them.

Public Square showing Euclid Avenue, Business Section.
Cleveland Sixth City

The city cars are wooden, double-truckers of the second generation. These buildings were replaced in the 1920's by the Terminal and Higbee's Department Store.

THE SQUARE, LOOKING WEST, CLEVELAND, OHIO.

The old Cuyahoga County Courthouse is at the corner of West Roadway (right background). The tall building next to it was built and occupied by the Cleveland Electric Illuminating Company. At the corner of Ontario Street stands the Old Stone (First Presbyterian) Church. This congregation has been located on this site since 1835, although this building was erected in 1855. Old Stone serves a denominational purpose, but also is a lecture and concert hall and provides Lenten services for those who work in the downtown area.

The streetcar shown here was one of the first partially steel vehicles operated by the Cleveland Railway Company beginning in 1913 (Series 1000). Note the new shelters with tile roofs for waiting passengers.

At center left is the Society for Savings Bank. East of the bank is the ornate home of the Chamber of Commerce. In the 1930's, the Chamber moved to more modern quarters and this building became Cleveland College of Western Reserve University. During the Depression and post-World War II era, this college enabled many young Clevelanders, especially those employed in the central business district, to earn undergraduate or graduate degrees. It specialized in job-related fields such as business administration, journalism, and social work. After the G. I. group moved on, classes were moved to the main campus on the east side; this building was razed.

Public Square, showing Post Office.
Chamber of Commerce and Society for Saving Buildings.
Cleveland

Dwarfed now by towering skyscrapers, this structure was designed to have its own style made up entirely of military and naval emblems inside and out, including the central column itself, which would be high above the busy plaza. The shaft is composed of ten blocks of Quincy granite and is seven feet in diameter at the base. The six bronze bands at the joints of the column name thirty prominent battles of the Civil War; inside are the names of those citizens of Cuyahoga County who served in that conflict. It was designed by Captain Levi Scofield and built in 1894.

Cuyahoga County Soldiers' and Sailors' Monument, Cleveland, Ohio.

This beautiful card, printed in Leipzig, was postmarked in 1905 and is unsigned. Superior Avenue, coming in from the west at the lower right, runs through the Square eastward. The post office is just under construction with a fence surrounding the excavation. The building with the mansard roof across East Third Street is the Case Block, leased to the city as city hall for many years. Beyond it is the tower of St. John's Cathedral. Across from the Case Block is the tower of the Hollenden Hotel. The tall white building in the center of the scene facing East Roadway is the Williamson Building, recently razed for the Standard Oil Building. In the center of the southeast quadrant is the Soldiers' and Sailors' Monument. The Park Building (right), which is under construction in this scene, was the first Cleveland building to use floor slabs of reinforced concrete. In 1850, this site was valued at $1,110 and was taken over by Mr. W. P. Southworth's store, a leading grocery firm.

Public Square. Cleveland, O.

No. 161   The Cleveland News Company, Cleveland, O.-Leipzig-Berlin

Trolley Tour

Anyone walking past the Soldiers' and Sailors' Monument on a pleasant summer day between 1902 and 1914 would likely have found a big open trolley car parked below the statue bearing the sign "City Touring Car." Its crew was seeking customers willing to pay 25 cents for a two-hour sightseeing ride around the city. In those days, trolley riding was a popular thing to do and a great way to see Cleveland.

2789—Residence Section, Euclid Avenue, Cleveland, O.

The men who became wealthy by their investments in Cleveland industry during the latter half of the nineteenth century established "Millionaire's Row" on Euclid Avenue between the Square and Case Avenue (East 40th). Our sightseeing trolley did not pass the part of the Avenue shown here but took a detour on Prospect Avenue. Residents were able to drive their carriages in the summer and their sleighs in the winter without having to deal with slippery rails or trundling cars.

Mayor Tom Johnson's Residence, Cleveland, Ohio

Tom Johnson was called "The Champion of the Common Man," and his political slogan was "Home Rule, Three-Cent Fare, Single Tax." Despite such populist sentiments, he made enough money on his street railway investments to build this great mansion at Euclid Avenue and Oliver Street (East 24th Street). He was both mayor and congressman.

TOM JOHNSON'S MONUMENT, CLEVELAND, OHIO.   10

This handsome, massive stone house "where Lionel works" gives an idea of the dwellings all along Euclid Avenue. The houses west of East 40th Street (Case Avenue) were generally larger than the Severance house and set farther back from the street. This house was built in 1898 on the northwest corner of Euclid Avenue and 89th Street. After the Severance family moved to the Heights, it became the temporary home of the Huron Road hospital

Severance Residence. Cleveland, O.

while it was moving from its namesake street downtown to a new location in East Cleveland. At that time (1940), this building was taken over by the Cleveland Health Museum, the first of its kind in the world. The emphasis in the early years was on exhibits and models, although there were lectures, film showings, and group tours. Many of the early exhibits came from the American Museum of Health in New York via the 1939 World's Fair as well as from individual donors. In 1945, an adjacent mansion was acquired, and modern wings were added.

John D. Rockefeller ready for an Auto Ride.

Cleveland's most prominent citizen in the latter half of the nineteenth century was John D. Rockefeller— industrialist, philan- thropist, and founder of Standard Oil Company. The Rockefeller mansion stood at the southwest corner of Euclid and Case (East 40th Street) Ave- nues. In later years, the family spent more time at the Forest Hill estate in East Cleveland. Many tales are told about this man. Russell Hehr's

grandmother told of Rockefeller giving out dimes to children outside the Euclid Avenue Baptist Church. On this unusual card, the wealthiest man in the world is being helped into his "duster" for a spin in his open touring car around 1910. Notice the lantern near the license plate, the huge fenders, and running boards. The lady in the back seat is probably his beloved wife, Laura.

Euclid Avenue, Garden Theatre, Cleveland, Ohio.

Eastbound trolleys swung back onto Euclid Avenue at East 40th Street and passed the Garden Theatre. Before the advent of air conditioning, outdoor or garden theatres were popular in the summer. They were built to "capture every breeze." Musical impresario Max Faetkenheur staged/produced operettas and other musical entertainments for the Euclid Avenue Garden. Tables in the garden were sheltered by huge umbrellas. However, the growth of vaudeville and movie theatres downtown proved to be too competitive, and eventually, the Garden gave way to commercial development.

Historical Bldg., Cleveland, Ohio

At the corner of Fairmount Avenue (East 107th Street) and Euclid Avenue stood two prominent and popular structures. This building of the Western Reserve Historical Society opened on the southeast corner in 1898. The site had been purchased and given to the society by the Chamber of Commerce so that it could use the former museum property on the Public Square. Organization of a predecessor group occurred in the 1850's. The building contained a library as well as many exhibits, paintings, drawings, maps, and other artifacts. In 1939, the museum and library moved to a mansion on East Boulevard. From 1902-1904, this building also served as the home of the First Unitarian Church.

The building with the tall chimney in the left background was the rear of the Beckwith Presbyterian Church, a forerunner of the Church of the Covenant. In later years, it served as the gymnasium for Case School of Applied Science.

On the northeast corner of East 107th Street and Euclid Avenue stood the Elysium—"the largest ice-skating rink in the world," measuring 100 by 300 feet. Built in 1907, it was in operation for three decades. "Elysium" is Latin for "a place of happiness." Popcorn king Dudley S. Humphrey, who built and owned it along with Euclid Beach Park, probably chose that name because of its classical style; he was said to be a rather academic type. During the winter months, afternoon and evening sessions offered live band music. School, college, and professional hockey teams all played here, including the Cleveland Barons. Many local and international contests were also held here. For a short while, the famous Gavioli band organ (later at the roller rink at Euclid Beach Park) was played here. The building was also used as barracks for both World Wars.

After 1945, the Humphreys pulled out and the professional hockey teams went elsewhere. Ownership of the land reverted to Case Institute of Technology, which owned it originally. It was used as a bowling alley and (later) a used car agency before being razed.

The tower in the distance (upper picture) is part of the Church of the Covenant.

Exterior of Elysium-Largest Ice Skating Rink in the World, Cleveland, Ohio.

Immediately east of the Elysium, east bound cars would reach the wye at University Circle. In this view an interurban is heading to the right toward the heights and its eventual destination of Cleardon. The large open city car on the left is seen approaching from East Cleveland and headed toward downtown.

This card dates from about 1908. One year later, complaints appeared in the press that the automobiles "swarming through University Circle" raised so much dust that paving would be desirable. The main building of Case School of Applied Science can be seen towering above Doan Brook, which ran beneath the row of trees between it and the Circle. Adelbert College of Western Reserve University occupied the building on the left.

University Circle, Cleveland, Ohio.

Garfield Memorial,
Cleveland
Sixth City

J. A. Garfield.

The left-hand route at University Circle brought sightseeing cars east on Euclid Avenue past the colleges to Coltman Road. At this point cars were routed over to Mayfield Road and up the steep grade toward Coventry. Eventually, a spur led into Lakeview Cemetery near Garfield's tomb. Over the years, many of the leading families of the city buried their dead in Lakeview. Included among the famous are John D. Rockefeller and his wife.

James A. Garfield was the nearest Cleveland could claim to having a native son in the White House. Born and raised in Mentor, Ohio, he was president of Hiram College, a congressman for sixteen years, and senator-elect from Ohio at the time of his nomination for the presidency. He also served with distinction in the Union Army during the Civil War.

The 180-foot-high Garfield monument was completed in 1890 at a cost of $225,000 raised by popular subscription. The design, by George Keller of Hartford, Connecticut, seems more Turkish than American. Behind this statue of the president are two of fourteen stained glass windows from the studios of Louis Tiffany. On a clear day, the whole northeast side of the city and a stretch of Lake Erie can be seen from the porthole-like windows in the tower.

One of the more prominent Cleveland families of the nineteenth century was the Wades. Jeptha H. Wade, Sr. pioneered the telegraph industry before starting the Cleveland Rolling Mills in 1863. Later, he became involved in banking and real estate, and built a mansion on Euclid Avenue across from the home of John D. Rockefeller. He was a member of the association that acquired the 200 acres in 1869 that became Lakeview Cemetery. In 1898, his grandson Jeptha H. Wade III had this chapel built in the cemetery in memory of his grandfather. Like the Garfield memorial, it was decorated in part by Louis Tiffany.

Wade Memorial, Lake View Cemetery, Cleveland, O.

Entrance to Forest Hill, Cleveland

From Coltman Road, a Euclid car traveled past Superior Road to the gatehouse of Forest Hill, John D. Rockefeller's famous estate. According to Grace Goulder's book *John D. Rockefeller: The Cleveland Years*, he purchased seventy-nine acres of land here that originally belonged to the Doan family, who gave their name to Doan Brook, Doan Street, and Doan's Corners. An association of investors was formed to develop the property as a "water cure and place of public resort," and a hotel was built.

Forest Hill, John D. Rockefeller's Residence, Cleveland Sixth City

Both the hotel and a "water cure" sanitarium failed, so Rockefeller bought the property for his exclusive use. He first attempted to operate it as a summer boarding house but finally decided to use it as a family summer home. He and his family "summered" there from 1878 to 1914. After Mrs. Rockefeller died, Mr. Rockefeller did not return from New York City, where he then resided. The house burned down in 1917. Later, part of the land became a public park.

Walking Tour I

Our first walking tour begins at West Ninth Street, goes out Superior Avenue to East 9th Street, proceeds north on East 9th to Lakeside Avenue, turns west, and ends just before West 6th Street on Lakeside. However, at no one time would all of the sights shown be seen since the postcards are dated over a period of two decades.

The central business district of Cleveland before 1900 was located on West Superior between West Ninth and Ontario Streets. The Perry-Payne Building at the left is obviously a carry-over from the ornate style of the Victorian era. The tall building down the street was built by John D. Rockefeller in 1905. The low buildings in the center are remnants of pre-Civil War architecture. Note the "Eclipse Finder" on the front of the street car. This was designed to catch any hapless person or animal that got in the way and "fend" them off the track. All Cleveland cars had them for several decades before the 1930 models came out.

Superior Ave., looking West, Cleveland, Ohio.

Ontario Street and Superior Avenue cross each other in the center of Public Square. The signs on the corner building advertise the Eastland (a lake steamer), Cedar Point (an amusement park near Sandusky), Anna Held Cigars, and the Home Dentists. The building in the shadow at the left is Forest City Hotel. The open bench street cars in this view probably belong to the "Little Con" Company—Cleveland City Railway—and are headed for East Superior or St. Clair. Behind these are a Lake Shore interurban and a closed city car.

The flagpole in this view was installed at daybreak on July 4, 1876, as part of Cleveland's celebration of the centennial. Made of Bessemer steel, it was 160 feet tall (replacing an earlier, eighty-foot pole that had been destroyed during a torrential rain in 1875) and the gift of prominent businessman Henry Chisholm.

This card was made in Germany for the Cleveland News. The message on the back is dated 9/4/09; the writer complains to his brother that he must pay $5.00 a week for board.

The Arcade is a covered thoroughfare connecting Superior and Euclid Avenues at about Fourth Street. This view looks south down the Arcade's four-hundred-foot "avenue" lined with shops on the ground floor. At the south end, a flight of steps goes up to the level of Euclid Avenue. Pedestrians using the Arcade are saved a climb up the grade on the east sidewalk of Public Square that is windy and very cold in the winter. There are four more levels under the grand glass roof, each lined with more specialty shops or offices. The author remembers Ito's Japanese store with its quaint and unique Oriental merchandise where his family liked to buy green tea. M. C. Yeagle, a one-time football star at Western Reserve, ran a store on the second level that sold "Sabbath school supplies" in the 1920's and '30s. The trusses holding the roof are hinged in three places, giving the appearance of a Gothic-style roof. At the base of each truss is a gargoyle from which people have reported flames shooting.

THE MAIN PUBLIC LIBRARY, CLEVELAND, OHIO.

This card is post-marked 1917, so the picture is obviously an architect's drawing because the library did not open until 1925. At that time, it had one of the most complete collections and the most up-to-date equipment of any public library in the country. Located on Superior Avenue between the Federal Building and the Federal Reserve Bank, it is another of the grand, monumental structures of which the establishment was very proud. It was designed to match the Federal Building; but when completed, it showed the soot and grime that covered the walls of its neighbor.

The *Leader* was founded by Edwin Cowles in 1854 as an anti-slavery, pro-Republican newspaper. Later, the *Evening News* and the *Sunday News-Leader* were added to newspaper stands. The *Plain Dealer* was the *New York Times* of Cleveland, both in style and party preference. This fine building on Superior Avenue at East Sixth is said to have boasted black walnut and marble interiors, and was completed in 1912.

The famous Hollenden Hotel was farther east on Superior Avenue. It was built in 1885 on the site of the home of James Farmer, which was also the birthplace of the Friends Church in Cleveland. The builder of the hotel was Liberty E. Holden, whose name had originally been spelled "Hollenden." Holden was publisher of the *Cleveland Plain Dealer*, which was published diagonally across Superior Avenue from this hotel for many years. It was the first hotel in the world to be built with electric lights, and it was also fireproof. Additions were made in 1920 with renovations made in 1946. Although it was once the largest hotel between New York City and Chicago, its final form was a smaller, more modern building in 1963.

The Hollenden Hotel, Cleveland, Ohio.

In 1927, Radio Station WJAY made its debut at the Hollenden with the aid of twenty-two batteries borrowed from taxicabs. One feature of this station consisted of programs directed to nationality groups. The Showboat Supper Club lay behind the large windows to the left of the main entrance. For many years, the Cleveland City Club met each Saturday at noon in the ballroom for lunch and a forum.

THE CLEVELAND DISCOUNT BUILDING.

East of the Hollenden Hotel is the Cleveland Discount Building (later, the NBC Building) and the Olmstead Hotel. The Discount Building replaced the Colonial Theatre, a leading legitimate house for many years.

The next intersection was East Ninth Street, originally one of the "Lakes" streets—Erie. Michigan and Champlain Streets were swallowed up by the terminal complex in the late 1920's. Superior, Huron, Ontario and St. Clair Avenues still exist.

2773 — Central Armory, CLEVELAND, O.

This massive castle-like structure at Lakeside and East 6th Street was built by the county in 1893 to house units of the National Guard, but it also was used for exhibitions and spectacles. In 1916, it was used by Charles Evans Hughes for his presidential campaign. The building was 122 feet wide and sported balconies. The exterior has echoes of Italian medieval municipal design; however, Schnauer and Schmidt were the architects. The fortress was demolished in 1965.

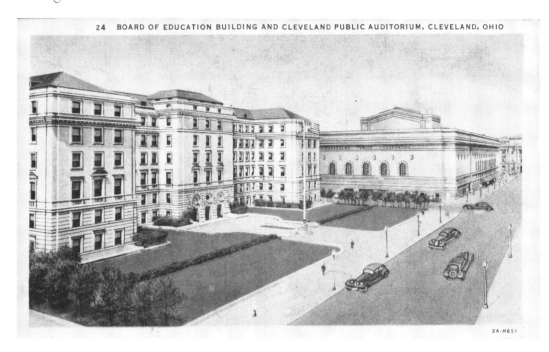

24 BOARD OF EDUCATION BUILDING AND CLEVELAND PUBLIC AUDITORIUM, CLEVELAND, OHIO

This beautiful building, considered to be part of the overall Mall development, was erected in 1930. Before that, the Board's headquarters on the same site at East 6th Street and Rockwell Avenue consisted of a red brick structure of typical Victorian school design. This had originally been the Rockwell School.

Using the armory for large gatherings was eliminated in 1922 with the opening of the Public Auditorium, which contained 11,500 seats that could be removed for exhibitions; a stage that was 72 feet wide and 42 feet high; and a five-manual pipe organ of 150 ranks with an echo division. There is also a music hall seating 2,500, another exhibition hall, and other meeting places. Industry, house, flower, and auto shows were held here as well as operas and circuses. In 1924, the Republican National Convention was held here and nominated Calvin Coolidge.

In 1870, Cleveland had 92,829 people; twenty years later, the population had almost tripled to 261,353—the tenth largest city. In 1920, it passed Baltimore to become the fifth largest city with 800,000 inhabitants. It dropped back to sixth in 1930 and, by 1940, had suffered a drastic drop when people moved to the suburbs.

The year 1920 also holds the record for streetcar riding, but that was the year J. P. Morgan is said to have decided that the automobile was here to stay and began transferring investments from traction companies to General Motors.

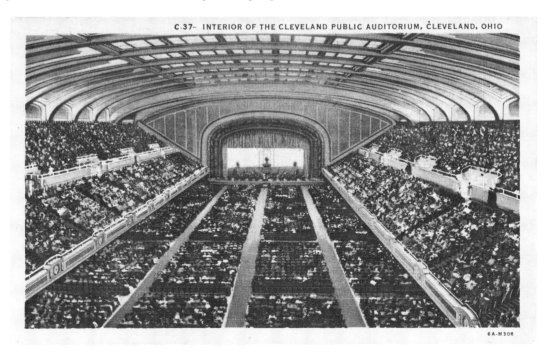

C-37- INTERIOR OF THE CLEVELAND PUBLIC AUDITORIUM, CLEVELAND, OHIO

The East Ohio Gas Company's Building, Cleveland, Ohio.

This corporate building fits in well with the public structures surrounding it. In 1915, it replaced a row of attached residences called the Park Row, which had been a fashionable residential center in the late nineteenth century. The site is at East 6th and Rockwell Avenue, a block north of Superior Avenue.

In 1912, the new Cuyahoga County Court House opened on Lakeside Avenue facing south toward Ontario Street. A few years later, the new City Hall, a building of similar size and appearance, opened at Lakeside Avenue opposite the Public Auditorium. These buildings plus the Federal Building and, later, the Public Library, were parts of a group plan for creating a spacious park-like area for all important public buildings—"The Mall." At the time of the photo, this steep slope of Lake View Park ended at the lake shore. Eventually, an extensive fill moved the shore several hundred feet to the north. Later, the East Ninth Street Pier was built on the fill and, still later, the Great Lakes Exposition was held on this land.

The New Court House as seen from the Lake.
Cleveland
Sixth City

Walking Tour II

This second walking circuit begins at Public Square, goes east on Euclid Avenue to East 18th Street, and returns by way of Prospect Avenue.

This famous eatery, located on Euclid Avenue just east of the Square, catered to downtown workers and shoppers for luncheon and dinner. If Ma and the kids came down to join Pa for dinner and a show, here was a family restaurant that they could enjoy. Self-service was reasonably fast, and the menu's variety was good.

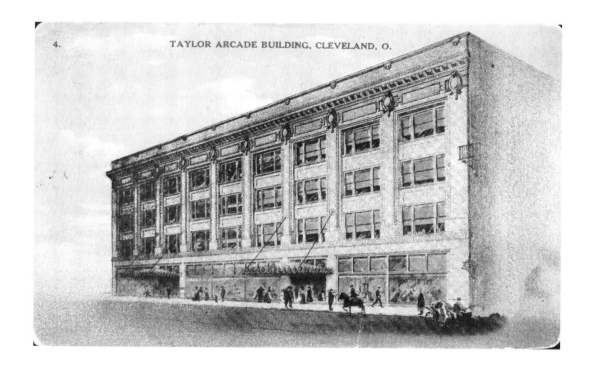

The original plan for Cleveland does not show Euclid Avenue. All the streets were laid out parallel to the lake shore, which runs in a southwest-northeast direction. When a through highway from Buffalo arrived, it came into the center on an east-west line. This road became known as Euclid Avenue after the township of Euclid. Superior Avenue was supposed to be the principal commercial street and, indeed, was during most of the nineteenth century.

One of the first business firms to begin the eastward move out Euclid Avenue was the store of William Taylor, Son and Company, which moved to this fine structure east of Fourth Street. Additional stores were added to the department store to create "Taylor Arcade." Taylor's was subdued and had no children's playroom, toy store, or escalators. It catered to the general public.

Just beyond Taylor's was the Hippodrome Building and Theatre. This large, ornate structure opened in 1908 and presented musicals, stage plays, operas, vaudeville shows, and (later) movies. There were entrances from both Prospect and Euclid Avenues. Its Victorian elegance is apparent in this view of the main stairway.

The Hippodrome was absorbed by the B. F. Keith enterprise, becoming its flagship theatre until the Palace opened in 1920.

GARFIELD AND NEW ENGLAND BUILDING,
EUCLID AVE., CLEVELAND, O.

This is an early view of the corner of Euclid Avenue and Bond Street (East Sixth). The Garfield Building, completed in 1897, was the first steel-framed office building on Euclid Avenue. Its name came from the builders, sons of President James A. Garfield. It later became known as the National City Bank Building.

This view looking south at the southwest corner of Euclid Avenue and East Ninth Street shows the Citizens Bank Building (light-colored building on the right), which was occupied until the 1920's by a bank of that name until it merged with others to form the Union Trust company. The facade of the building was remodelled to provide retail stores; the huge Doric columns, carved from solid stone, became surplus. The building on the corner, the Schofield Building, housed many physicians in its heyday. Its elevators were open cages with shaft windows lighting up the vast spaces in which riders were precariously suspended—or so it seemed to the author when he was a child. The third building on the extreme right was the Hickok Building, which housed the local branch of the Bond Clothiers on the ground floor.

Photo. only, Copyright 1905 by the Rotograph Co.
G 1879a   Citizens and Schofield Building, Cleveland, O.

This picture of the Statler Hotel on the corner of East 12th Street and Euclid Avenue could have been taken in Boston, Buffalo, or New York City. Mr. Statler seemed to have a standard plan as well as a standard slogan: "We sell sleep."

The Statler, along with the Hollenden and the Cleveland, were the leading first-class hotels in the city. Investors evenutally bought this beautiful building and converted it into an office complex.

This excellent, German-made card shows the home of the Union Club, founded in 1872, at East 12th Street and Euclid Avenue. William Ganson Rose, Cleveland historian, wrote that it "became one of the most important social organizations in the west, uniting men of influence and ambition as an intellectual force in the community. From the Union Club stemmed much of Cleveland's future greatness."

Upper Euclid (from East Ninth Street through Playhouse Square and on to about East 18th Street) was the area of stores and theaters that catered to more affluent citizens. Typical of the fine establishments was Sterling and Welch. Located just beyond the Union Club, it sold furniture and house furnishings. At Christmas time, a tall tree was erected in this court and amply decorated.

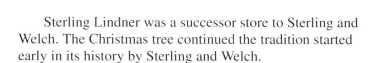

Sterling Lindner was a successor store to Sterling and Welch. The Christmas tree continued the tradition started early in its history by Sterling and Welch.

EUCLID AVENUE, LOOKING WEST FROM EAST 13TH STREET, CLEVELAND, OHIO.

This card shows the center of the fashionable shopping area. The first building at the right was the home of Higbee's Department Store. A Cleveland-owned business, it later moved to the Terminal group and still stands on Ontario Street between the Public Square and Prospect. The grayer building beyond it was the home of Sterling and Welch. On the left of the street is the main part of Halle Brothers, also a Cleveland-owned, high-class department store. It extended back through two blocks. In later years, it was bought by Marshall Field of Chicago. Beyond Halle's was the Cleveland Athletic Club.

This card is postmarked 1949, but the autos appear to be of 1920's vintage. In a few years, they would drive the streetcars out.

PLAYHOUSE SQUARE.

East from 13th Street is the triangle formed by the intersection of Euclid and Huron Avenues, and East 14th Street—commonly called "Playhouse Square," a row of first-run movie houses and a legitimate theatre. On the right is the Hanna Building, owned by a successful family that provided industrial and political leadership to Cleveland and the nation. Out of sight on 14th Street is the entrance to the Hanna Theatre, a long-time home for Broadway shows.

High-class specialty shops occupied the retail stores along Euclid Avenue. Before the Public Library opened on Superior Avenue, it was located on the upper floors of one of the buildings on the left.

The streetcar shown here was designed by Peter Witt, a one-time Cleveland traction commissioner. Developed by the Cleveland Railway Company, it became a standard design for Cleveland and was copied throughout the country and the world.

B. F. KEITH'S PALACE, CLEVELAND, OHIO.

No one walking out Euclid Avenue before World War II should have passed this magnificent structure without attending a show. The author remembers being impressed by its great size and elaborate decorations while seeing a vaudeville show starring Sophie Tucker. A matinee cost as little as 35 cents and included five vaudeville acts, a feature film, serial episode, comedy and newsreel. Fortunately, this building has now been restored after a long period of darkness.

The marquee in this photo is on Euclid Avenue. Just west of the Keith Building is the sign for Loew's State. First-run Hollywood productions were scheduled for the Palace, the State, or the Allen (farther down Euclid Avenue just out of camera range). The marquee beyond the State with the horizontal signboard was the Ohio—a beautiful legitimate theater that shared Broadway productions with the Hanna.

One block south of Playhouse Square on East 14th Street is the intersection of Prospect Avenue with Bolivar Road. (Spanish-speaking visitors must be astonished to hear the name of their great South American leader pronounced "Bahl'-i-verr.") This scene shows the two buildings that dominated the intersection for decades. One is Gray's Armory, built by a private military organization known as the Cleveland Grays in 1893. It was used for public events as well as military activities. The unidentified church building at the left was the home of the First Unitarian Church from 1880 until 1912 when that congregation moved to outer Euclid Avenue. This building was then used by Grace Episcopal Church, which offered free pews when it was organized in 1845.

GRAY'S ARMORY, CLEVELAND, O.   10667

Farther west on Prospect Avenue is the Y. M. C. A. When this building opened in 1891, it was the first structure purposely designed to be a "Y." Financed by Sereno Fenn and John D. Rockefeller, it contained a gymnasium, auditorium, marble swimming pool, and an electric elevator. The opening of the 22nd Street "Y" only 31 years later demonstrates the rapid growth of people's interest in self-improvement.

The intersection of Prospect, Huron and East Ninth Street was planned to be the "New Center"—a "Great White Way" with theatres, restaurants, and night clubs. At the extreme lower right corner, the marquee of the Empire Theatre can be seen. On the right is the Caxton Building, designed by Frank S. Barnum, built during 1901-1903, and used by commercial printing and graphic arts trades. The building with the tower is the old Y. M. C. A. building built in 1891 with money raised by popular subscription. The building beyond the "Y" that is shaped like a flat-iron is the Osborne Building, built in 1898. In his book on Cleveland landmarks, Clay Herrick writes that this was the only exclusively medical building in downtown Cleveland. When Rudolph S. Orgler remodelled the building in 1956, he featured its 120 bay windows. The Rose Building is on the left.

A closer look at the Rose Building reveals a sign at the bottom corner reading "The New Center." The Rose Building was built in 1900 by Benjamin Rose, president of the Cleveland Provision Company and a well-known philanthropist. At that time, it was the largest office building outside of New York City. It was dubbed "Rose's Folly" because it was on the outskirts of town. For many years, it was occupied by dentists and is now the headquarters of Blue Cross. Many visitors and Clevelanders remember the Forum Cafeteria on the Ninth Street side.

The Colonial Hotel stood on Prospect Avenue just east of Sheriff Street (East 4th). This view shows the whole expanse of Prospect as far as East Ninth Street. The tall building at the end of the row (center left) is the Rose Building. The Guardian Building (originally called New England), which faced south on Euclid Avenue, can be seen directly behind the Colonial. An arcade connected the hotel with Euclid Avenue.

The Colonial Arcade was built in 1898 to make it convenient for guests of the Colonial Hotel on Prospect Avenue to patronize stores and theatres on Euclid Avenue. Note the skylight. Since 1910, when this postcard was made, the arc lamps have been replaced by electric lights and a new floor installed.

Interior of the Colonial Arcade Cleveland, Ohio.

New West Side Market House, Cleveland Sixth City

The walking tour out Euclid Avenue and back down Prospect has now brought us to within a half-block of Ontario Street. The trip could easily be completed by returning to the Public Square. Adventurous walkers could walk south on Ontario Street, cross the Central Viaduct and Abbey Avenue Bridge to reach the West Side Market. It was built in 1910 and operated by the city, along with at least two other markets. Privately owned markets included one at Euclid Avenue near East 105th Street, one on Superior Avenue near East 118th Street, and the Sheriff Street Market.

Public Parks

9342   WATERFALL IN WADE PARK CLEVELAND OHIO

In the early decades of the nineteenth century, Clevelanders loudly protested against proposals to pave streets, put in sewers or lights, or establish schools and parks. In 1836, however, land was donated along the lake front by interested citizens and called Clinton Park. A hotel was constructed there—a "cool lakeshore resort far from the heat of the city" all the way out at what became East 17th Street.

But when the Cleveland and Pittsburgh, and the Cleveland, Painesville and Ashtabula Railroads built lines to the water's edge, Clinton Park gradually succumbed to smoke and noise. It was still shown on a map in 1892, but the only large park in that year was Wade Park.

Wade Park was Cleveland's first major park. Newell Samuel Cozad, who lived on some 100 acres as a young man, decided that part of that land should be kept in its natural state as a park. It was located north of Euclid Avenue, east of Doan Brook. But financial reverses forced Cozad to sell his property to industrialist Jeptha H. Wade, an artist who made a fortune in the development of the telegraph system. Wade began to develop the land as an estate, although he allowed part of the site to be used as a public park. In 1882, the city council accepted 1,100 feet of his property extending north from Euclid Avenue that Wade offered to them for a park.

Dam in Wade Park, Cleveland Sixth City

This view of the Wade Park Lake looks south. The Centaur statue is at center left. Doan Brook continues its flow over the dam and on toward Lake Erie.

Wade Park Lake. Cleveland Sixth City

This view is from the dam along Doan Brook looking south across the lake toward the Amasa Stone Memorial Chapel of Western Reserve University. The chapel was the gift of Stone's daughters, Mrs. Samuel Mather and Mrs. John Hay. It was erected in 1910.

Mr. Cleveland at Wade Park, Zoo.   Cleveland, Ohio.

In 1885, a zoo opened in Wade Park, which increased attendance. The zoo expanded in 1889 when J. H. Wade gave more animals to the collection and an octagon building was built to house them. In 1890, cable cars on Hough Avenue arrived from the Public Square at the west entrance to Wade Park at Doan Street. This provided another route in addition to the Euclid Avenue line on the south and Wade Park Avenue on the north.

THE CLEVELAND ART MUSEUM AT WADE PARK, CLEVELAND, OHIO.

When Jeptha Wade gave Wade Park to the city, he held back a tract called the "college reservation" that his grandson later donated for the Cleveland Museum of Art. John Huntington and Horace Kelley contributed the money for its construction, and The Hinman B. Hurlbut Trust set up an endowment for its operation. This postcard view is dated 1916, soon after the museum opened. The white marble facade appeared severe except for the Doric portico and the lesser pavilions at each corner. After World War II, extensive additions were made on the west and north sides; but the original neo-classical facade was kept intact. The fine arts garden was planted in the 1930's.

One of the museum's early permanent exhibits was the Armor Court—always a big attraction to school children.

212—Aerial View of Fine Arts Gardens, showing Art Museum and Severance Hall, Cleveland, Ohio

University Circle has been referred to as an "American Parnassus" and the center of culture in Cleveland. The street going from the middle foreground of the scene diagonally toward the right center is Euclid Avenue. The street going diagonally toward the left center is Chester Avenue, and the street curving around toward the top left by the lake is East Boulevard. Clockwise from the left are Epworth-Euclid Methodist Church, Cleveland Museum of Art, Flora Stone Mather College of Western Reserve University, Severance Hall, and (lower right) the Amasa Stone Chapel of the University.

Severance Hall, home of the Cleveland Symphony Orchestra, was built in the southeast corner of Wade Park. Opening in 1931, it was designed by the Cleveland architecture firm of Walker and Weeks, and seats 1,844 persons in the large concert hall. A smaller chamber music room seats 400. It was a gift of John L. Severance in memory of his wife, Elizabeth DeWitt Severance. John D. Rockefeller, Jr., also contributed to its construction.

18   SUN DIAL AT FINE ARTS GARDENS SHOWING SEVERANCE HALL, CLEVELAND, OHIO

Russell Hehr remembered going to the orchestra programs for school children. He recalled the Egyptian style of the foyer with its red jasper columns with gilded capitals, and the silver and blue floral pattern of the ceiling. He thought the console looked like an organ; it actually controlled the colored lights that changed patterns constantly to match the mood of the music.

ROSE GARDENS IN WADE PARK, CLEVELAND, OHIO.   282

Flowers replaced Wade Park's animals after they were moved across town to Brookside Zoo when the Cleveland Museum of Art was built on the site. The Rose Garden's setting was lovely, especially in the summer, and perfect for Sunday afternoon walks.

High Bridge in Wade Park,
Cleveland, Ohio.

Sometimes, families in the neighborhoods north of Wade Park Avenue would pack a picnic supper and walk to the Wade Park picnic area. Crossing this bridge, kids would stomp heavily on the plank floor or stoop to peer through the cracks. These fashionably dressed young ladies are standing near the spot where jugs could be filled with spring water.

In 1867, land was purchased for Lake View Park. During the 1870's and 1880's, drives, walks, fountains, and small lakes were made; bands performed; and it became a popular place for outings and picnics. An iron picket fence separated the park from the railroads. This 1906 view shows the wide expanse of grass and trees where people could get away from the heat of the city (just over the crest) and enjoy a cooling lake breeze. As the population moved away from downtown and more industry moved in, Lake View Park was neglected. In 1898, only a small vestige of it remained behind the present day location of City Hall.

Lincoln Park, Cleveland, Ohio.

According to Cleveland, *The Making of a City*, a tract of land on Jennings Road was purchased by a Mrs. Pelton in 1850 as a site for a girls' school and park. Her goals were not achieved, and the land lay idle for years. The people in the area thought it should be used for a public park and kept tearing down the fence. Finally, the city purchased the land in 1879 and landscaped it. It was called South Side Park until 1896 when it was named Lincoln Park after renovation. This 1911 scene indicates that it was a popular place.

Since 1865, William J. Gordon, wholesale grocer and mayor of Glenville, purchased tracts of land fronting Lake Erie and bordering Doan Brook in Glenville, converting them into a beautiful estate. When he died in 1892, his will

Gordon Park Boulevard, Cleveland, Ohio.

directed that the 122 acres become a public park. The title passed to the city of Cleveland on October 23, 1893, upon conditions that the name be known as Gordon Park, the lakefront be protected, the drives and ponds be maintained, no fence obstruct the lake view, and the city preserve the Gordon burial lot. In 1894, the picnic grounds (thirty acres) adjoining the park were purchased from the Gordon family.

Before the Lake Front Highway was built, Lake Shore Drive began at the north end of East 72nd Street. It went down to the shore, made a right angle turn past the bathing beach, and proceeded east through Bratenahl to connect with Lake Shore Boulevard.

ENTRANCE TO ROCKEFELLER PARK, CLEVELAND, O.

In 1896, John D. Rockefeller gave 276 acres of Doan Brook land for a parkway from the north end of Wade Park to Gordon Park. One lone horse pulling a sulky seems to be the extent of traffic on the lower drive by the Wade Park Avenue Bridge on this card, dated August 19, 1907. This was one of three stone arch bridges built with a grant given in 1900 by John D. Rockefeller; the other two were at Superior and St. Clair Avenues.

Bathing at Gordon Park Beach, Cleveland *Sixth City*

The major attraction of Gordon Park in its early years was the bathing beach on Lake Erie. The combination dance hall and bath house shown here was built in 1901. A 1940 pamphlet called *A Chronicle of Cleveland* states: "[In 1901] construction was begun to increase sewage disposal into the lake, coincident with construction of bath houses at Gordon and Edgewater Parks. Bacteria welcomed bathers!" It was two or three decades later warnings of "germs" in the water of Lake Erie near the city were heard, and people began transferring bathing activities to points clearly east or west of the city.

A lot of the people in this picture, dated 1911, must have walked a considerable distance to reach this spot. It was not until 1914 that the East 79th Street car line opened to a pedestrian tunnel near the entrance to Gordon Park. Note their woolen bathing suits—heavy when wet, itchy in the sun, and very slow to dry.

River Scene in Gordon Park, Cleveland *Sixth City*

Doan Brook flowed into the Lake at Gordon Park. According to the statement on the back of the card, over 200 boats were anchored here during the summer months. These craft seem to be quite modest compared to those found in a modern marina.

100961

A number of modern apartment hotels began appearing in the city after World War I. The Sovereign was similar to Wade Park Manor, Park Lane, Fenway, and Commodore—all in the East 105th Street-Euclid Avenue area.

LITHUANIAN GARDEN, ROCKEFELLER PARK, CLEVELAND, OHIO—18

From 1818 when a schooner brought six Irish families to Cleveland until the present, people with a variety of ethnic backgrounds have moved to Cleveland. Beginning in 1926, an organization called the Cleveland Cultural Garden League began creating gardens in Rockefeller Park to honor the people and cultures of these different nations. This Lithuanian garden, designed in the form of a lyre, is typical. The original leadership of this movement was provided by two newspaper men—Leo Widenthal of the *Plain Dealer* and Charles Wolfram of the *Jewish Independent*. William Ganson Rose called the string of gardens "an excellent course in international relations."

When Cleveland's leaders finally began to develop a public park system, they included all sections of the city. Consequently, the Wade-Gordon-Rockefeller system on the east side was paralleled by Brookside and Edgewater on the west side.

Whereas Wade Park tended to cater to the arts and letters with its gardens and museums, Brookside was designed to meet peoples' needs for natural science and sports. The zoo, which had been an early attraction at Wade, was moved to Brookside in 1907. This large brick building was crowded soon after it was built with animals on exhibit and humans inspecting them. It was a real advancement over the wooden octagon at Wade.

Most popular with the younger generation was Minnie. With children astride, she led the annual Fourth of July parades and was a "must see" for every visitor.

Baseball is in progress at Brookside Park in this 1906 scene. The valley of Big Creek is not only deep, but wide and provided ample flat land for baseball and other athletic activities. Judging by the crowd of men, women, and children both on foot and in buggies, this must have been an important game. Brookside was the center of games played by the amateur teams of the Cleveland Baseball Federation. In 1932, the Fulton Road Bridge connecting Fulton with Memphis Avenue cut across the park; while it is a handsome structure, it divided the space in two. In the 1960's, Interstate I-71 was built through the park, destroying much of the land used for recreation.

Brookside Park offered recreation for everyone. Boat rental to row around the large, shallow lake was available by day or evening. This photo was likely taken on the Fourth of July. Adding a festive note, Japanese lanterns are hanging on the large trees growing on the "islands" in the lake. A gas lamp for night illumination stands on the little island in the center; the ladder used by the lamplighter can be seen leaning against a tree in front of it. This large crowd may be gathered on the lake shore for a boat race or some other water entertainment.

Holiday scene; Brookside Park. Cleveland, O.

Edgewater Park is located on the edge of Lake Erie. In 1889, the West and South Side Citizens League formed to promote the development of the resources of those parts of Cleveland lying west of the Cuyahoga River. As a result, land for parks was sought. Jacob Perkins had a farm extending west along the shore from the foot of Waverly

Entrance to Edgewater Park.

Avenue (West 58th Street) that he sold to the city in 1896. A boulevard was constructed from a point near Detroit and Pearl Streets to this property. It later became Bulkley Boulevard. After streetcar service was extended to this area in 1902, Edgewater became a very popular place to swim or dance for many years.

Bathing at Edgewater Park.

This spot seems to be popular with swimmers and non-bathers alike. At the crest of the bank is the right-of-way of the old Lake Shore Railroad with its multi-armed telegraph poles. This line is still in service, carrying Conrail and Amtrak trains.

Euclid Creek, Cleveland, O.

Euclid Creek in Metropolitan Park is near what was the eastern end of the Euclid Avenue car line. It was a handy place for the author's seventh grade teacher to take her class for a hike and picnic in 1925. The site had been used to quarry blue sandstone since the 1850's. The demand for building stone declined about the time the expanding urban area began to encroach on this still-open land.

LAKE IN GARFIELD PARK, CLEVELAND, OHIO.

In the 1920's, Garfield Park was a popular place for school and church picnics. There was plenty of space for softball games and other group activities. Small lakes were a part of most Cleveland parks and the one in Garfield Park was a favorite place—in a day when recreation was more quiet and relaxed than now.

Prior to the completion of the Baldwin Reservoir in 1925 and the Kirtland Pumping Station in 1927, many people found the chlorinated, unfiltered Lake Erie water both unpalatable and unsafe. City-wide delivery routes for Distilata water flourished. (The City Ice and Fuel Company had a market plan that kept its delivery wagons and, later, trucks busy all year long: ice in the summer, coal in the winter, and distilled water at all times.) But pure spring water in Garfield, Wade, and Rockefeller Parks was free; everyone brought a jug and queued up for pleasant-tasting water. Many just stopped for a quick drink after walking or bicycling in the Park.

MINERAL SPRINGS AT GARFIELD PARK, CLEVELAND, O.

A PRETTY SPOT IN GARFIELD PARK, Cleveland

The scenery is pretty and so are these two young ladies dressed in their Sunday best. People went promenading in that era—not running or jogging.

Nathan Ambler, a dentist who established his practice in Cleveland in 1852, built a house overlooking Doan Brook in an area that became known as Ambler Heights. In 1894, Mrs. Martha B. Ambler gave 25 acres between there and Cedar Avenue to the city. With some additional land, the construction of Ambler Parkway along Doan Brook south of Rockefeller Park began. It wound up the hill connecting with what became North Park Boulevard and the Shaker Lakes. Obviously, it was a grand place for a buggy drive on a Sunday afternoon. Soon, it became possible to drive all of the way from Shaker Lakes through Ambler Boulevard, past University Circle, through Wade and Rockefeller Parks to Lake Erie at Gordon Park.

Overlook Road, Euclid Heights, Cleveland, Ohio.

This scene looked much the same well into the 1920's. Euclid Heights was the name given to a development as well as to a street. Since 1897, the destination board on the streetcars that went out Euclid Heights Boulevard read "Euclid Heights"; thus, many people may have thought it was a municipality.

East 82nd, one of Cleveland's Beautiful Streets, Cleveland, Ohio.

There were scores of streets throughout the city that looked similar to this in the years before and after World War I. This section was located in the neighborhood between Euclid and Superior Avenues, and between East 115th Street and about East 55th Street. Old timers may remember the poplar trees that were planted along many of the streets. As the trees grew, their roots played havoc with the sewer system, so they were cut down and replaced with more benign species, such as maple, just after World War I.

Amusement Parks

As the city park board began to develop public beaches at Gordon and Edgewater Parks, business-minded promoters realized that people could easily be persuaded to spend their recreation money on things besides rent for a dressing room. So amusements and games, good drinks, and rides were added to Manhattan Beach at East 142nd Street and Lake Erie to entice crowds. Because traffic fell off on Saturday afternoons and Sundays, electric railway companies throughout the United States bought or established amusement parks along their routes. The Cleveland Electric Railway Company purchased Manhattan Beach, changed its name to White City, and built a loop into the grounds. Its terminus was Euclid Beach Park. Animal shows and a tea room were among the attractions of White City.

A major activity at White City was the "Shoot-the-chutes." A boat with wheels and filled with squealing riders hurtled down the grade into the lagoon at the bottom. Everyone was slightly dampened by spray, and a great time was had by all.

The fate of White City is inscribed on this card: "This entire place burnt down yesterday." The buildings were never rebuilt, although a dance hall and bathing beach were used for some years. The place eventually became the site of the Easterly Sewage Treatment Plant.

40:—AERIAL VIEW OF EUCLID BEACH PARK, CLEVELAND, OHIO.

D. S. Humphrey was a creative, idealistic, and enterprising business-man. He started out as a farmer; one of his principal crops was popcorn. In 1893, he founded the Humphrey Company as a retail popcorn business. He established a popcorn stand on Cleveland's Public Square in 1895. By 1899, he became so successful that he was able to acquire Euclid Beach Park at East 163rd and Lake Shore Boulevard. He proceeded to eliminate what he considered to be "dubious" attractions. He arranged with the Cleveland Electric Railway to reduce street car fares by eliminating the surcharge to the beach.

ENTRANCE TO EUCLID BEACH, CLEVELAND, OHIO.

Old timers will recall this streetcar loop into Euclid Beach Park with a station by the pony track. Cars of the best-remembered route began at Luna Park, went across town to St. Clair Avenue, and then out to Euclid Beach. Many groups chartered special cars to take them on outings to the park; the cars in this scene are from one of the first groups of double-truck cars appearing at the turn-of-the-century. Many of them lasted well into the 1920's. As the automobile increasingly took over traffic, trolleys were finally moved to a flat loop adjacent to Lake Shore Boulevard.

SCENIC RAILWAY AT EUCLID BEACH PARK, CLEVELAND, OHIO

The Scenic Railway that wandered over a wide area of the park began its journey in this Grand Central Terminal. Each train made four completed circles of the track area. The train pictured here is entering the second floor of the station on the inside track. It also went through the station on the outside track and through the tunnel in the center foreground of this photo.

Scene at Euclid Beach, Cleveland, O

The Euclid Beach campground to the east of the main park could be seen by riders on the Scenic Railroad. There were lots of tents and small buildings.

CONCRETE COTTAGE, EUCLID BEACH PARK.

Cleveland
Fifth City

Humphrey's "campground" evolved into a more resort-like development with the construction of substantial cottages like this one. A sedan from about 1919 is parked at the right.

A trip in the Figure 8 at Euclid Beach Park, Cleveland, Ohio.

The Figure 8 was one of the earliest, shortest, and tamest of Euclid's roller coasters. The control of roller coasters was by shoulder-high levers such as these. The two older riders in old-fashioned workclothes look rather dour to be out having a "great" time, but the well-dressed boys and the two employees also look rather glum.

BIRD'S EYE VIEW OF BIG COASTERS, EUCLID BEACH PARK, CLEVELAND, OHIO.

Two trains started out together on the double-tracked Derby Racer. As they went up and down the made-made hills, one train would be ahead and then, the other. Everyone tried to guess which train would arrive back at the terminal first. The Thriller had the highest pinnacle and most abrupt decline; as they looked ahead into an abyss, riders were sure that the structure had been removed and the train was about to go into free-fall.

FINEST CAROUSAL EVER MADE, EUCLID BEACH, CLEVELAND, OHIO.

The same claim was probably made by many amusement parks throughout the world for its major attraction: the carousel. These rides were popular with everyone except twelve- to sixteen-year-old boys, who considered them too tame. These horses were marvels of wood carving; their construction was and still is an art form.

When the hanging cars on this tower were first used, they were called "flying boats." The "boats" were about the same as the rockets but looked like they might have been imported from Venice. Centrifugal force spread the "boats" farther out from the tower as they picked up speed.

This is a typical large-group picnic scene such as might have been pictured at the spring outing planned by the Mayflower Congregational Church of East Cleveland. In its May-June issue of 1929, The *Mayflower Messenger* urged: "Let's all go to the Mayflower Picnic. The place selected is Euclid Beach Park, which can be easily reached by all, and at very little expense. The time . . . is Friday afternoon and evening, June 14th. . . . At 3 o'clock the big time will begin with games, contests and stunts . . . prizes being given to the successful contenders. At five o'clock free tickets for selected amusements will be issued to all Mayflower boys and girls, thirteen and under, and strips of tickets at reduced rates furnished to all. . . . From six to seven there will be a picnic dinner, families bringing their baskets . . . as they may wish. A large section of tables, in a good location will be reserved. A good orchestra has been engaged for the evening and the Lodge reserved exclusively for Mayflower families."

THE LOG CABIN, EUCLID BEACH PARK, CLEVELAND, OHIO.

This is the building called the "Lodge" and is where the "orchestra that had been engaged" played. The fox trot was the most popular dance; but waltzes were played, and German-American grandparents at the Mayflower picnic probably insisted on appropriate music for a Schottische.

Euclid Beach was one of the few parks with no admission charge, ticket prices for rides and activities were low, and streetcar fares ranged from five to ten cents. Fifty cents would buy quite a meal of popcorn, hot dogs ("frankfurters"), golden ginger ale, and ice cream sandwiches.

EUCLID BEACH — BATHING SCENE, CLEVELAND, O. 1907

This German-made card shows children well-dressed (like adults) for a dip in Lake Erie at Euclid Beach.

Despite the encumbrance of skirts and shirtwaists, these ladies seem to be having a great time doing a little boating. The pier remained as seen here for a long time.

THEATRE, EUCLID BEACH PARK, CLEVELAND, OHIO.

As a change from active sports, bathing, dancing, or skating, people could go to a movie. Before World War I, moving pictures were a novelty. After 1918, large movie houses began to appear. This building bridged the gap. The small building in the lower right looks like a ticket booth; these were scattered throughout the park.

ROLLER SKATING RINK, EUCLID BEACH, CLEVELAND, OHIO.

The Humphrey Company catered to its more energetic customers with a summer roller skating rink at Euclid Beach and an ice-skating rink at the Elysium in the winter. The Gavioli band organ first seen at the Elysium is in the center of this card.

The importance of dancing at Euclid Beach can readily be seen by the size of the pavilion. The success of Euclid Beach was due in part to its good, clean, family-oriented environment. Churches and Sunday Schools were among the organizations patronizing the park. One card stated: "No intoxicating liquors sold here." Everyone knew this to be true even after repeal. The

Dancing in the Pavilion, Euclid Beach Park, Cleveland, Ohio.

dance hall was always clean, polished, and well-maintained. The orchestra was always high class; and the refreshments tasty and inexpensive. A couple bought a strip of tickets at ten cents each and walked out onto the floor at the beginning of each dance, relinquishing one ticket to the attendant. At the end of the number, the ushers walked out from each side, each one pulling an elastic cord until they met in the center, gently pushing everyone off the floor.

Automobile Day at Euclid Beach Park,
Cleveland, Ohio.

Harry Christiansen, the authority on Cleveland transportation, states that this scene took place in 1909. The models shown are primitive. In 1916, the Cleveland Automobile Club promoted the idea that on this day each year, its members would each bring a carload of orphans to Euclid Beach Park. This event became a custom through the years.

Watching the Aviators at Euclid Beach.

Cleveland
Sixth City

Seven years after Kitty Hawk, aviation was still an exciting wave of the future. The lake shore was an ideal place to view an air show; here is one in progress. This may be the famed flight by Glenn Curtiss from Euclid Beach to Cedar Point and back. He achieved the "fantastic" speed of 32 m.p.h. By sponsoring events such as this, welcoming the automobile to its gates, and building a movie house, Euclid Beach encouraged the forces that eventually put the local amusement park out of business.

In 1951, trolley service to Euclid Beach was discontinued after just over half-a-century of operation. Movies, radio, and television contributed to changing lifestyles; and this wholesome, family-oriented park declined in use. The park closed in 1969, and the land was used for a high-rise, apartment development.

Luna Park was advertised as Cleveland's "gayest outdoor amusement center." For a quarter-of-a-century, the huge crescent atop the elaborate entranceway could be seen for miles from its position high above Woodhill Road. Trolleys bringing patrons to Luna Park could be identified by a wooden crescent mounted under the right front window that was marked "Luna Park."

The forested, family-picnic atmosphere of Euclid Beach was a great contrast to Luna Park with its Oriental flair. It looked like a near-Eastern bazaar with Chinese pagodas thrown in. All of the usual carnival attractions were available: games of chance, freak shows, distorting mirrors, dark passageways. Apparently, the management was not as interested as the Humphrey's were in maintaining a "wholesome" tone. But crowds loved it, and the place was very popular for over 25 years.

Shoot the Chutes, Luna Park, Cleveland, Ohio.

The most prominent and probably most popular attraction in Luna Park was the "shoot-the-chutes." Note the sign on one of the low buildings at the left reading: "Infant Incubator, 10 cents." The square building with the Russian style towers was later replaced by a roller rink that outlasted the rest of the park by a decade.

Luna Park was a popular place for conventions. In 1916, the A. F. L. held a Labor Day celebration that brought 50,000 people to Luna. These young men in their baggy bathing suits may have been attending some such function.

Motorcycles can be seen racing around a banked track before a large crowd of spectators. Changing patterns of population distribution, alternative methods of amusement—radio, motion pictures—plus the flexibility of travel by automobile caused a rapid decline in the popularity of Luna Park in the late twenties. It closed in 1929, and the site became the location of a large housing project during the New Deal days.

Baseball Park, Cleveland, Ohio.

What old-timer does not fondly recall League Park, sometimes called Dunn Field, where Babe Ruth and Tris Speaker played? It was located off the beaten path at Lexington Avenue and Dunham Street (East 66th) because Frank Robinson, who owned a streetcar line, also owned the "Spiders," a National League team. Like an amusement park, a ball park was a good supplier of patrons to a streetcar company. The Spiders performed so badly that they were sold to St. Louis. The park was sold to the owner of the "Naps," an American League team that became the "Indians." They played here until the lake front stadium was opened in 1931.

The highlight year was 1920, when the Indians won the World Series from Brooklyn before a crowd of 27,000 inside and hundreds more on rooftops of adjacent houses.

The streetcar in this scene was of the 1100-1200 series, the work horses of the Cleveland Railway system for forty years.

113 View from Terminal Tower, Looking Toward Lake Erie, Cleveland, Ohio

This 80,000-seat stadium opened on July 31, 1931, with a game between the Indians and the Athletics (Philadelphia - 1, Cleveland - 0). Obviously an improvement over League Park with better parking and seating, it is municipally owned and used for football, boxing, and many other events as well as baseball.

Schools, Universities, Churches, and Hospitals

Two rival Cleveland businessmen promoted competing, but neighborly, colleges in the 1880's: Case School of Applied Science, sponsored by Leonard Case, and on the adjacent tract to Case, Adelbert College, which moved to Cleveland from Hudson, Ohio, at the urging of Amasa Stone. The college was named after his son who had died while a student at Yale University; it later became part of Western Reserve University. In the 1960's, these two schools merged to become Case Western Reserve University. Leonard Case was instrumental in developing the forerunner of the Pennsylvania Railroad while Amasa Stone was an early promoter of the Lake Shore Railroad (later, the New York Central). These two systems also eventually merged in the 1960's, becoming Penn Central and, later, Conrail.

This aerial view of the Case campus was made in the twenties. The white building with the tall chimney behind the Case main building was part of the Western Reserve University Medical Center. The long building just above right center was the home of the Cleveland School of Education. Operated by the Cleveland Board of Education, it included an observation school where future teachers could watch classes in action. The various buildings of Case extended to the right from "Old Main" along the bluff above the valley of Doan Brook. The street winding along its bank beneath the trees was Lilac Drive and was, indeed, lined by lilac bushes. The square, light-colored building at the right above the School of Education was the home of the Lincoln Moving and Storage Company. The steep slope leading up to Cleveland Heights extends across the pictures above all the buildings.

Case was among the earliest independent institutions devoted to technical education such as Rensselaer, M. I. T., and Stevens. It was the first school of this type not located on the Eastern seaboard. It took a long time for industrialists to appreciate and demand trained engineers; but once started, they thoroughly supported such institutes and their students. The growing electrical industry soon made a separate instructional building necessary. In the 1920's, buildings were also devoted to physics, chemistry, and mechanical and mining engineering.

The expansion of mining in the United States and elsewhere during the last half of the nineteenth century was phenomenal, and education in this industry became a necessity. By 1930, however, it had ceased to be a growth industry, and Case discontinued its program.

After decades of suffering some snobbish remarks by its rivals for being only a "school," Case changed its name to Case Institute of Technology in 1946. Still later, it merged with its neighboring institution to become Case Western Reserve University.

Mining Building, Case School of Applied Science. Cleveland, Ohio

In the teens and twenties, the entire freshman class of Case was transported by a special Pennsylvania train to this camp near Waynesburg. It was thought that every engineer, regardless of his later specialty, should have hands-on experience in surveying and map-making. Although portable buildings were used later on, this experience in "roughing it" was not universally valued by the participants, including faculty members who were assigned to the project.

ADELBERT COLLEGE, CLEVELAND, OHIO.

Although John D. Rockefeller made a contribution to the purchase of the land for the two colleges and also gave money to build the physics building at Case, his major contribution to higher education in America was funding he supplied to the University of Chicago.

Dormitory Bldg., Adelbert College, Cleveland, Ohio

The second building to be built on the Adelbert campus was this splendid three-story structure, in 1882. Located to the south of Adelbert Hall, it housed the president and his family, and provided dormitory rooms for students. (Imagine the reaction today of a candidate for university president upon being told that living quarters would be provided next to those of the students.) This building had two names: "Cutler" and "Pierce."

Following a trend set by two other Ohio colleges —Antioch and Oberlin—Western Reserve experimented in co-education. This produced such a dispute that a policy of segregation by sex was adopted. In 1892, this building on Bellflower Drive and one other facility were opened to accommodate the growing number of female students. Linda

Guilford House of the Woman's College, Cleveland, Ohio

No. 1866. National Art Views Co. N. Y. City.

Thayer Guilford, after whom this building was named, was a well-known Cleveland teacher. Mrs. Samuel Mather (Amasa Stone's daughter) was one of Miss Guilford's pupils and contributed substantially to its construction.

CLEVELAND SCHOOL OF ART, CLEVELAND, O   10688

This artistically designed building opened in 1905 to carry on the work of the Cleveland School of Art founded in 1882 as a result of efforts by the local art club. The Art School was located on Juniper Road near the Art Museum and, thus, adjacent to the other colleges.

Life for young people in the city may not have been very different in 1910 from today; the writer of the postcard reports that he has not forgotten his cousin Martha but has just been "so busy working in the daytime and going to parties at night."

Central High School, Cleveland, Ohio.

Originally located in a basement on Prospect Avenue in 1846, Central High School moved to lovely tree-shaded Willson Avenue in 1878. Considered the "finest high school in the West," it was attended by many of the city's leading citizens, including Laura Spelman, who became Mrs. John D. Rockefeller. Many early civic leaders opposed using taxpayers' money for high school education. Some referred to the original Central High as a "piece of vicious extravagance."

With a budget in 1852 of $900, it was hailed by supporters as "good enough for the rich, cheap enough for the poor."

The first high school football game was played on October 25, 1890, between University School and Central. University won by 26 - 0. In the spring, they played again, and Central came out on top by 10 - 3.

Although the state allowed only one high school in the city at that time, a branch of Central was opened in a grade school on the west side in 1855. In 1861, it became West High School. This building on Franklin Boulevard opened in 1903.

This building was the high school for East Cleveland. When the western part of East Cleveland township was annexed to the city in 1873, its high school became the third in the city—East High School.

With the central part of the city, the west side and the east side supplied with high schools, the south side was last with South High School.

It is obvious that all four of these schools were built about the same time and, apparently, were designed by the same architect. It was an effort to keep up with the growth in number of students: there were two high schools in 1890 granting 62 diplomas; in 1915, there were nine schools awarding 370 diplomas.

TECHNICAL HIGH SCHOOL, CLEVELAND, O   10686

With the introduction of manual training in 1884, interest in more technical courses rather than the traditional liberal arts program led to the introduction of high schools devoted to industrial arts, vocations, and applied sciences on both the east and west sides before 1910. Their emphasis can be illustrated by the action of the principal of East Tech, Pliny W. Powers, in 1935: he ruled that every student in every class should study some aspect of the automobile because of its importance to modern life.

Entrance to Ursuline Convent. **Nottingham, O.**

Although early settlers in the Western Reserve were Protestant New Englanders, the Irish and other European Catholics began to settle here as early as 1818. The Ursuline Sisters came to Cleveland from France in 1850 to help establish Catholic education for the area. The Ursuline Academy was founded in 1877; the St. Joseph Seminary for boys, in 1887.

Caring for orphans was a big business in the mid-nineteenth century when this institution was established on Woodland Avenue. Lower death rates, smaller families, and the greater availability of foster homes has changed the picture. The Jewish Orphan Asylum later moved to University Heights.

2776 Jewish Orphan Asylum, Cleveland, Ohio.

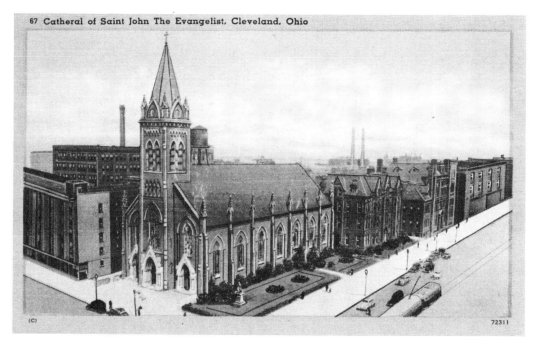

67 Cathedral of Saint John The Evangelist, Cleveland, Ohio

Over the years, other Catholic institutions were built along Superior Avenue as far as East 12th Street: the rectory, the chancery, St. John's College, and an auditorium. In 1946, Archbishop Edward Hoban began rebuilding the cathedral and other buildings to follow a pattern of harmonious architecture. The complex became known as Cathedral Square. The old building was encased in Tennessee sandstone, its interior was redesigned, and the tower relocated and enlarged. Officially called the Cathedral of St. John the Evangelist, this newly refurbished landmark was dedicated on November 7, 1952, by Bishop Ammadeus Rappe.

Glenville Congregational Church
Cor. Eddy Rd. and St. Clair Ave.
Cleveland, Ohio

Not all churches were large and fashionable. Glenville Congregational, organized and built in the first decade of this century, follows a style that was most common throughout the United States—duplicates can be found almost anywhere. This neighborhood was developing rapidly at the time.

The Reverend Karl Owen Thompson, who came to Glenville Congregational Church as pastor in 1912, had the lower left "flat" in this building on Eddy Road as his parsonage. This is where the author lived when he arrived in Cleveland at the age of six months

Trinity Cathedral, Cleveland, Ohio.

This Episcopal cathedral is English Gothic, in contrast to St. John's Roman Catholic cathedral, which demonstrated French influence (even though most of Cleveland's nineteenth century Catholics were German or Irish). The ushers here wore striped trousers, cutaways, and carnations in their buttonholes. The congregation that became the nucleus for Trinity parish began meeting in 1816. The church was incorporated in 1828, became the diocesan cathedral in 1890, and completed this magnificent building in 1907.

This picture must have been taken in 1907 or soon after because the stone is still clean and white. The two residences to the east are the first two mansions in "millionaires' row." Businesses began invading lower Euclid Avenue in the 1890's, but the "row" east of Trinity Cathedral lasted until about 1915 when streetcars were allowed on Euclid Avenue east of 22nd Street.

Cathedral chairs distinguish this chapel from a parish church that would have had pews. Not only was Trinity noted for its architectural features, but its music under the direction of Edwin Arthur Kraft was outstanding.

First Church of Christ, Scientist, Cleveland, Ohio 69

70106

The fifth branch of the "mother church" of Christian Science in Boston was established in Cleveland in 1888. This church, in turn, planted many branches in the metropolitan area. In 1931, it built and occupied this landmark structure overlooking the university area from the crest of the Heights; some say it symbolizes the dominance of religion over the purely rational or Christian Science over the secular variety.

The Tifereth Israel Congregation followed its members as they moved eastward from the East 55th Street neighborhood. The original building later became Mount Zion Congregational Church, an important center for black Christians. The magnificent near-Eastern-style building shown here has been a landmark overlooking Wade Park since 1924. Rabbi Abba Hillel Silver was an important spiritual leader in the Jewish community, Cleveland civic affairs, and world Zionism.

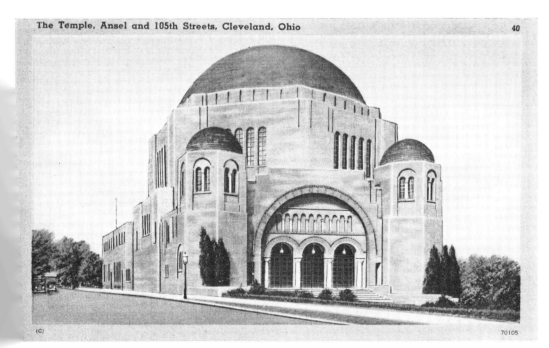

The Temple, Ansel and 105th Streets, Cleveland, Ohio 40

70105

Cory Methodist Church, 1117 East 105th Street, Cleveland, Ohio   37

78301

    Judging from the time that the area north of Superior was developed, this fine structure was built just before or after 1900. The 1992 Cleveland telephone directory lists Cory as still doing the Lord's business at the same address.

·

    St. Vincent Charity Hospital was the first general hospital organized in Cleveland and was founded as wounded soldiers returned from the Civil War.

Charity Hospital, Cleveland, Ohio.

Lakeside Hospital, Cleveland, Ohio.

This large building was located on Lakeside Avenue east of East Ninth Street. The first hospital on this site opened in 1866. In 1931, Lakeside moved to a location in the medical center at Western Reserve University far from the side of the lake.

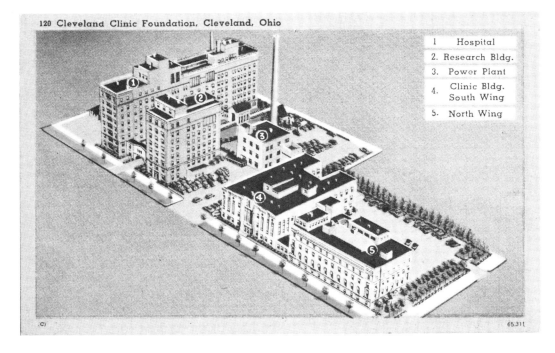

120 Cleveland Clinic Foundation, Cleveland, Ohio

1	Hospital
2.	Research Bldg.
3.	Power Plant
4.	Clinic Bldg. South Wing
5.	North Wing

The Cleveland Clinic was founded in 1921 by Dr. George W. Crile and others. It was located at Euclid Avenue and East 93rd Street.

Newburgh was an early rival of Cleveland to become the leading city in northern Ohio. By the 1870s, Cleveland had won the race and annexed its southern neighbor. While Newburgh thrived on industry and railroads, its image was based on the location of the state mental hospital. As late as the 1920's, it was still referred to by its 1855 designation as the "Northern Ohio Lunatic Asylum" or simply the "Newburgh Insane Asylum."

In 1896, land belonging to this institution was combined with adjacent farmland to create Garfield Park.

Business and Industry

1. THE OHIO BELL TELEPHONE CO., GENERAL OFFICE BUILDING.

CLEVELAND, OHIO.   106356

Called a "temple to telephony," the Ohio Bell Building opened in 1927. The equipment that led to the conversion of Cleveland's telephones to dial operation was included. The building on the left is the Caxton Building.

Rockefeller Building, Cleveland, Ohio.

Postmarked in 1913, this card shows the building constructed by the Rockefellers in 1905. In the 1920's, it was known as the Kirby Building before the Rockefellers regained control of it and changed its name back to the original.

POST OFFICE AND U. S. CUSTOM HOUSE, CLEVELAND, OHIO.

This beautiful building opened in 1911 at a cost of over $3,000,000. It was part of the Mall—a planned group of public buildings including the City Hall, the Courthouse, and the Library; a lake front union station was also planned but never started. The exterior was granite, and the white statues consisted of two groups by Daniel Chester French: "American Commerce" and "American Industry."

INTERIOR U. S. POST OFFICE, CLEVELAND, OHIO.

New Central Y. M. C. A., Prospect Avenue and East 22nd Street,
Cleveland

    Growing cities everywhere attracted young men from the country to work in stores and factories. This fine building, opened in 1912, provided those without local relatives or friends a place to stay, engage in athletics, and to study both religious and secular subjects. The Y. M. C. A. evening classes developed into a complete program; similar to the modern community college, it emphasized professional and technical subjects. Eventually, Fenn College was created by the "Y" and moved out of this building to its own facility on Euclid Avenue.

    At the extreme right is St. Vincent Charity Hospital.

G 1871   Sheriff St. Market House, Cleveland, Ohio.

Before the days of the supermarket and shopping center, market houses with stalls rented to individual sellers were popular with consumers seeking fresh food from the farmer or the fisherman—and lower prices. There were a number of these operating in Cleveland in the early decades of the century. One of the largest and best known was the Sheriff Street (East 4th Street) Market House, built and operated by a private corporation. On opening day in 1891, beef steak sold for $.15 per pound.

It is interesting that a building designed for the plebian purpose of supplying food should have been so elaborate. The central part had a great domed skylight at its center; there were 312 stalls inside connected to utilities by conduits under the aisles. The veranda over the sidewalks protected merchants from the weather. In 1930, a five-alarm fire destroyed a large part of the building.

Coal came up on railroads beginning in the early 1850's from mines in southern Ohio, Kentucky, and West Virginia. Much of it was used by the iron and steel industries in Cleveland, although some of it was sent on ore vessels to be used in plants on the upper lakes. This is one reason Cleveland has been called "the best location in the nation." It is also a center of population and can ship finished goods to cities in the Ohio Valley and the entire Great Lakes area.

Iron Industry, Cleveland, O.

Note the old-fashioned steam-powered switch engine. Its tender bears the name "River Terminal Railway Company," one of several industrial lines in and around the city. The first railroad to connect Cleveland with the Ohio Valley was the forerunner of the "Big Four," the Cleveland, Columbus, and Cincinnati. This line was completed to Columbus in 1851 where it connected with Ohio's pioneer line—The Little Miami Railway, bound for Cincinnati. Later, it had its own line. It acquired the "Bee Line" to Indianapolis and St. Louis, and eventually became part of the New York Central System. In 1852, the Cleveland and Pittsburgh Railroad was finished to Wellsville on the Ohio River. Soon, the Cleveland and Mahoning Valley; the Cleveland, Lorain and Wheeling; and the Wheeling and Lake Erie lines were built. All did a good business in coal and ore.

Detroit has been known as the "motor city," Akron as the "rubber city," and Pittsburgh as "steel city." Cincinnati makes soap and Milwaukee makes beer. What is done in Cleveland? Iron and steel—the flats along the river were sometimes referred to as "Manchester" after the famous steel city in England. But according to Rose (p. 993), Cleveland was the fifth U.S. city in value of manufactured products in 1939, making cars (Chandler, Winton, Stearns, Jordan, and Peerless), light bulbs (Nela Park), paint (Sherwin-Williams and Glidden), street cars (G. C. Kuhlman), and other products. In 1939, there were 2,330 manufacturing establishments with steel mills being the most distinctive.

7274. A STEEL PLANT CLEVELAND OHIO

American Ship Building Yards, Cleveland, Ohio.

The growth of the steamship business on the Great Lakes stimulated shipbuilding. Almost every town had at least one firm engaged in this activity and in Cleveland shipbuilding was one of its major industries.

Industry does not have to be ugly; one example is Nela Park. The founders of the National Electric Lamp Association wanted "to establish a better working environment in order to develop a unique morale." In 1911, the first of these buildings on the bluff above Euclid Avenue in East Cleveland was opened. Called the "University of Light," the grounds did, indeed, look like a college campus. Most of the engineers and executives lived in the general area. School children were conducted through parts of the plant where exhibits and demonstrations described the progress of research in the field of lighting. Eventually acquired by the General Electric Company, one of the memorable features of Nela Park was the annual display of Christmas lights on its buildings and throughout its grounds. As the note on the back of the card says, "[Nela was the] Lighting Headquarters of the World."

C 45—The New General Electric Lighting Institute at Nela Park, Cleveland, Ohio

Great Lakes Exposition

EXPOSITION BUILDING, CLEVELAND

The most famous exposition in Cleveland was in 1936, but it was not the first one. In 1908, these modern-looking structures appeared across Lakeside Avenue from the Central Armory, which also contained exhibits. The theme extolled the accomplishments of Cleveland's manufacturers during the preceding five decades. Visitors came from all around and, it is said, at least one group decided to bring a new plant to Cleveland. The city hall was built on this site in 1916.

MAIN ENTRANCE TO THE GREAT LAKES EXPOSITION, CLEVELAND, OHIO   16

The 100th anniversary of the incorporation of Cleveland as a city occurred in 1936. Although progress had been made in bringing the economy out of the Depression, there was still much unemployment and memories of all the sufferings that people had endured since the 1929 crash. William Ganson Rose and others conceived the idea of launching an exposition in Cleveland. Not only would it commemorate the centennial, but it would "revive the spirit of civic pride and restore prosperity." Thanks to the cooperation of many people in industry, commerce, government, and cultural institutions, The Great Lakes Exposition was organized in a mere eighty days.

The Main Entrance was located west of the Public Auditorium and north of St. Clair Avenue. Thus, it could be easily reached from Public Square and Union Terminal using public transportation.

GL-128   RADIOLAND, GREAT LAKES EXPOSITION, CLEVELAND, OHIO

7A-H1792

Radio, which had become popular during the twenties, had grown in scope and acceptance during the early thirties. It was not surprising, therefore, to be confronted immediately upon entering the Exposition Grounds with "Radioland," an open air auditorium and band shell sponsored by the Sherwin-Williams paint company. Concerts as well as performances by well-known radio personalities were held here frequently.

GL10   COURT OF PRESIDENTS AT NIGHT, GREAT LAKES EXPOSITION, CLEVELAND, OHIO

The two rows of gilded eagles lining the bridge represent the sixteen presidents that came from states bordering on the Great Lakes: from Illinois, Abraham Lincoln; from Indiana, Benjamin Harrison; from New York, Martin Van Buren, Millard Fillmore, Grover Cleveland, Chester A. Arthur, Theodore Roosevelt and Franklin D. Roosevelt; from Ohio, William H. Harrison, Ulysses S. Grant, Rutherford B. Hayes, James A. Garfield, William McKinley, William H. Taft, and Warren G. Harding; and from Pennsylvania, James Buchanan.

GL2   AUTOMOTIVE BUILDING OF THE GREAT LAKES EXPOSITION, CLEVELAND, OHIO

Descending from the Bridge of the Presidents, people were confronted with the huge Automotive Building, which was actually two parallel buildings with an open space between. The automotive exhibits were summer-long auto shows. The newest model cars plus marine and other kinds of internal combustion engines were displayed. There was also an antique steam-powered car borrowed from the Smithsonian Institution as well as a dream car of the future—1950.

Proceeding north from the Automotive Building brought exposition-goers to the Hall of Progress, which showed how the world had progressed in the century since Cleveland became a city. The hall's architecture was significantly "modern." Inside were exhibits of utility companies and makers of home appliances displaying their latest achievements. The federal government had a pictorial presentation of its "New Deal" achievements and regular service, including a special post office.

At the edge of the lake was the ship that Admiral Byrd used to go to the South Pole.

On the slope from the base of the Stadium down to the shore of Lake Erie were gardens and a building housing exhibits of garden clubs and suppliers of gardening products. People had a respite from walking and looking by having tea at tables on the roof of this structure. They could relax and enjoy the lake breeze.

GL14 HORTICULTURE GARDENS ALONG LAKE ERIE, GREAT LAKES EXPOSITION, CLEVELAND, OHIO

6A-H1381

When tired of exhibits, a party of fair-goers could walk to the crowded, glittering Midway. Penny arcades, beer gardens, shooting galleries, freak shows, an Indian village, and "Spook Street" were among the many attractions. Off to one side was a nudist camp, Parisian dancers, and an exhibit called "The Story of Life"—all were quite in contrast to 19th century prudery.

SCENE OF THE MIDWAY, SHOWING CROWD, GREAT LAKES EXPOSITION, CLEVELAND, OHIO 83

"STREETS OF THE WORLD" AND GOODYEAR BLIMP LANDING FIELD,

GREAT LAKES EXPOSITION, CLEVELAND, OHIO   84

For those who still had strength left after walking through the Midway, the Streets of the World beckoned. This was a tribute to the many ethnic groups that contributed to the development of industry in Cleveland and the Great Lakes region. There was a Hungarian Sandwich Shop, a British Coffee Shop, an Italian Spumoni Shop, and a Syrian Souvenir Shop. There was ample evidence of a bubbling melting pot in Cleveland: A. E. Bates ran the Spanish Restaurant; Mrs. M. B. Steele, the Czech Jewelry Shop; and Abe Greenbaum ran the German jewelry store and the religious goods store in the Italian Village.

At the far end of the Streets of the World was the Goodyear blimp, which took visitors for rides.

GL 38: HIGBEE TOWER AND FLORIDA EXHIBIT, GREAT LAKES EXPOSITION, CLEVELAND, OHIO

Higbee's "Tower of Light" not only promoted its department store (recently moved to the Terminal area on the Public Square), but offered clothing and souvenirs for sale. Its art deco architectural style was considered "avant-garde" in 1936. An orange grove and an old-time Southern plantation were reincarnated at the Florida exhibit to promote tourism.

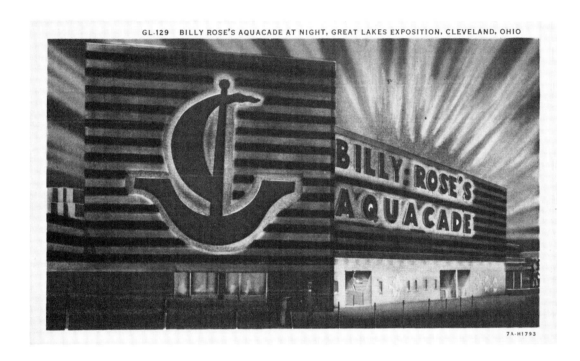

GL-129 BILLY ROSE'S AQUACADE AT NIGHT, GREAT LAKES EXPOSITION, CLEVELAND, OHIO

7A-H1793

If industrial progress in the Great Lakes States and Canada was the reason for the Exposition, pure amusement contributed greatly to its profits. Billy Rose opened this 5,000-seat open-air theater for the second season in 1937. On a floating stage were dancing, singing, and other musical acts. In the water were all sorts of swimming shows.

Waterways and Lake Steamers

LAKE ERIE AS SEEN FROM CLEVELAND YACHT CLUB.

The lake was the basis for the development of industrial Cleveland in the nineteenth century. Its natural beauty was often abused in the name of progress, especially along the shore between Edgewater and Gordon Parks. But after the construction of the Lake Front freeway, pride in the appearance of the city began to take hold. Today, Lake Erie has come into its own aesthetically as well as economically, although the quality of the water still leaves something to be desired.

Cleveland Harbor from Top of Rockefeller Building, Cleveland, Ohio.

In the center of the harbor is an ore-carrier and left of center is the gap in the stone breakwater for the river entrance. On each side of the channel are small lighthouses. The tower of the old Union Depot is directly north, and a railroad yard extending into the lake is behind it.

At the right is the sign for "Root and McBride," a large wholesale dry goods firm. Bank Street (West Sixth) is at right center. St. Clair Avenue is at the bottom of the picture with a horse and wagon, and a group of pedestrians. The Hoyt Building faces St. Clair Avenue at the extreme right; it was built in 1875 and had the first hydraulic elevator in the city. The second building from the left facing St. Clair is the Worthington Hardware Building, built in 1874 using iron framing. George Worthington founded the firm in 1829 to provide tools to dig the Ohio Canal. In 1988, almost all of these buildings were gradually being renovated and put to new uses. Today, the Main Avenue Viaduct runs across the area at the extreme left.

Scene along the Cuyahoga River.

A passenger ship is seen here steaming briskly down the Cuyahoga River toward the lake. Behind it are the wharves where such vessels docked prior to 1915. The skeleton of the Rockefeller Building under construction can be seen at the top of the rise.

Dear Rose, this is the place we landed coming home. Your Friend, Flossie Walck.

Scene along the Ohio Canal, Cleveland Sixth City

The opening of the Ohio and Erie Canal from Akron to Cleveland in 1827 helped propel Cleveland from a hamlet of 600 people toward its modern industrial greatness. In 1832, the canal opened all the way to Portsmouth on the Ohio River, linking Cleveland with the Ohio and Mississippi valleys, and the Gulf of Mexico. Traffic from the Eastern seaboard came to Cleveland by the Erie Canal through New York State and then across Lake Erie by steamboat. Other water-borne traffic came into Ohio on an extension of the Pennsylvania and Ohio Canal, and connected with the Ohio and Erie.

Although the canals were highly successful, movement on them was slow. Within thirty years, the railroads had taken over shipment of freight and carrying of passengers. The canal continued to be used for commerce and recreation for many years. Sections of it can still be seen today along the Cuyahoga Valley between Cleveland and Akron.

STR. CITY OF DETROIT III   D & C NAVIGATION CO.

Beginning in the 1890's, lake travel became so popular that steamers increased both in numbers and size. *The City of Detroit III* of the Detroit and Cleveland Navigation Company was built sometime around 1910. These "boats," as they were called, were propelled by huge paddle wheels on each side. During the 1920's and '30's, overnight trips to Detroit and Buffalo were promoted to vacationers by encouraging them to bring their autos on the boat with them. Thus, they could save a day's driving if headed for points beyond the steamer's destination.

Old-timers remember other vessels of the D & C line: *City of Cleveland III*, *Eastern States*, and *Western States* as well as the two largest and most modern steamers, *Greater Buffalo* and *Greater Detroit*.

With its sister ship *Western States*, the *Eastern States* was a workhorse of the Detroit and Cleveland Navigation Company. At various times, these "twins" provided service between Cleveland and Detroit, Detroit and Buffalo, and Detroit and Chicago. After the *Seeandbee*, one of the larger D & C "boats," (technically, they were ships) was converted into an aircraft carrier, the *States* carried on.

The most celebrated ship on the Cleveland and Buffalo line and the most famous on Lake Erie was the *Seeandbee*. From 1913 to 1938, she not only provided overnight service from Cleveland to Buffalo (alternating with the *City of Buffalo*) but was used for excursions from Buffalo, Cleveland, and Detroit to Mackinac and Chicago. In 1942, she was converted to an aircraft carrier, renamed *Wolverine* and used by the Great Lakes Naval Station to train pilots during World War II.

In the days before fast food, dining while travelling on either train or steamer was a first-class affair. This beautiful dining room abroad the *Seeandbee* played a major role in the cruise-takers' enjoyment.

Other boats of the C & B line were the *City of Erie*, *State of Ohio*, and *Goodtime*. The latter went daily to the amusement park at Cedar Point and the historic site at Put-in-Bay Island. At one time, steamers of this line went directly across Lake Erie to Port Stanley and Erieau in Ontario.

THE MAIN DINING ROOM OF THE GREAT SHIP SEEANDBEE, C. & B. LINE, CLEVELAND, OHIO.

One product of the Cleveland shipbuilding industry was the steamer *Eastland*. It was a popular ship; and for many years prior to 1914, it provided daily excursions in season from Cleveland to Cedar Point and ran moonlight cruises. On July 24, 1915, it was receiving passengers at the Clark Street bridge dock in Chicago when it overturned and drowned 812 people.

Steamer Eastland.

Union Terminal and Rail Station

In 1916, O. P. and M. J. Van Sweringen, developers of the residential community of Shaker Heights, bought the Nickel Plate Railroad (over 500 miles in length) in order to acquire a five-mile-long right-of-way through Cleveland to bring an electric rapid transit railway from Shaker Heights to the Public Square. The "New Union Station" shown here was part of their plan.

When finally completed, the Cleveland Union Terminal had a 52-story tower and seven huge arches instead of one. In 1929, it was the tallest building in the U.S. outside of New York City and attracted many visitors to its observation room near the top. But the Tower became only a part of a vast complex that included Higbee department store, office buildings, parking garages, and a new post office. Total cost was around $180,000,000.

The New Union Station, Cleveland, Ohio.   Hotel Cleveland.

The Terminal Tower has dominated Cleveland's skyline for over sixty years. Its offices, hotel rooms, and stores are still in use. It could be said to be a terminal for riders on the rapid transit lines since Amtrak now uses a small depot near the lake. Obviously, its builders did not anticipate the decline of rail use. Regardless, the Union Terminal project made Cleveland a leader in urban development and provided its citizens with a modern outlook that carried it optimistically into the mid-century.

INTERIOR OF UNION TERMINAL STATION, CLEVELAND, OHIO

This ticket lobby, located at a lower level than Public Square, was reached by ramps and stairways. In the center of this view is the information desk and clock. To the right, a traveler can be seen standing in front of the ticket windows. In the main concourse is the first of several entrances to the train tracks below. Above the heads of the waiting passengers is a bulletin board where roller signs announce the next departure and the destinations for which a train was bound. Many shops and a Fred Harvey Restaurant were behind and to the left of the camera in the concourse.

204—Aerial View of Downtown Cleveland, Ohio, Showing Terminal Tower and Terminal Group

Before construction of the Terminal complex could begin, the Cleveland Union Terminal Company had to acquire the land within a huge triangle as seen in the lower section of this postcard. It is bound by Huron Road (bottom), Superior Avenue (lower left corner), and Ontario Street (lower right corner). To make this transformation, about 1,400 structures were demolished between 1920 and 1930 when the project was completed.

80 HOTEL CLEVELAND, TERMINAL TOWER AND U. S. POST OFFICE,

CLEVELAND, OHIO

The last of the Terminal group to be completed was the post office, finished in 1934. The web of steel girders beneath it carried the catenaries powering the electric locomotives hauling trains in and out of the terminal. Mail arriving or departing by train could be brought quickly to the same place.

This arrangement did not last long. Before the station opened, 94 passenger trains left Cleveland each day in 1922. The station began operations in 1930; by 1932, 78 trains departed per day, eighteen of them operated by railroads that did not use the Union Terminal. In 1964, there were only sixteen daily departures from Cleveland. After Amtrak took over in 1971, no trains departed from the city. Eventually, Amtrak restored the once-famous Lake Shore Limited but its station was a temporary one near the lake front.

Penn. Square Corner E. 55th Street and Euclid Avenue.

Cleveland
Sixth City

This is a view of the Pennsylvania Railroad Station located on the corner of Euclid Avenue and Willson (East 55th Street) before the tracks were elevated. It was a well-designed brick and white stone building with a lot of open space around it. Since this depot could be readily reached by streetcar or carriage from both the fashionable and not-so-fashionable parts of the east side, it was widely used. The Pennsylvania continued to operate from this station until it abandoned passenger service.

Bridges and Airports

Along the Cuyahoga River, Cleveland Sixth City

Because most transportation was by water, commercial and industrial firms settled along the Cuyahoga River until the 1870s. Early horse-car lines had to negotiate steep grades to move from east to west or vice versa. The trans-valley viaducts have done much to knit the city and its activities together.

SUPERIOR ST. VIADUCT, CLEVELAND, OHIO.

West of the central span that swung open for ships with tall masts on the Cuyahoga River, the viaduct was constructed of stone. East of the center span, the construction was of steel.

High Level Bridge and Flats showing Cuyahoga River, Cleveland, Ohio.

A more sweeping view of the industrial area known as the "flats" is shown in this scene of the Detroit-Superior High Level Bridge, which replaced the old viaduct in 1917. This span was a double-decker with four streetcar tracks on the lower level. When trolleys finally disappeared, the lower deck was taken over by trucks.

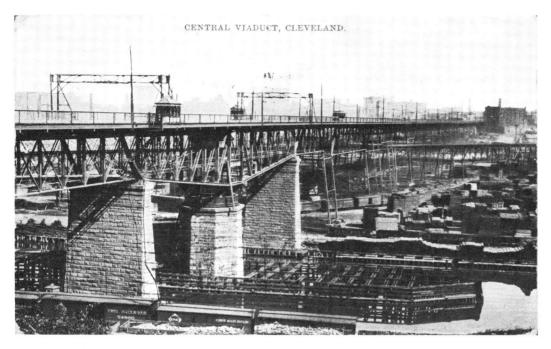

CENTRAL VIADUCT, CLEVELAND.

The Cuyahoga Valley continues on upstream as does the industry in the flats and on adjacent bluffs. The second viaduct to open was the Central in 1888. In 1895, the draw shown here was open when a streetcar fell into the river, killing a number of people. The Cleveland and Mahoning Valley Railroad—an early line into Cleveland from Warren and Youngstown—became part of the Erie. Some of its boxcars can be seen at the bottom of this view. At the upper right running at an angle to the viaduct, is a lower bridge, the line of the Nickel Plate. This road was built by speculators in the 1880's and eventually became the basis for the Van Sweringen empire.

When visitors came to Cleveland from non-industrial places, the Clark Avenue Bridge was a good place to take them to see what the steel industry really looked like. Several plants could be seen from the viaduct. The Clark Bridge trolley took workers to stairway entrances that led down from the bridge to the level of the valley. Flat cars shunting about could be seen carrying red-hot ingots from one part of the process to another.

CLARK AVENUE BRIDGE. LONGEST SPAN IN THE COUNTRY.

Cleveland
Fifth City

19 Lorain-Carnegie Bridge and Union Terminal, Cleveland, Ohio

During the streetcar era, Public Square was the hub of transportation and, hence, of business of Cleveland. In 1930, the Terminal brought rapid transit and inter-city rail lines to the same place. But even as the Terminal was being built, another project was under way that threatened the importance of the Public Square. The Lorain-Carnegie Bridge was begun in 1927, financed with an $8,000,000 bond issue. In 1932, it connected the Heights to the east by extensions of Carnegie Avenue with the new Airport and West Park by a widened Lorain Avenue; thus, it began to divert automobile traffic away from the old city center. Undoubtedly, it was also a factor in attracting people away from public transit and into their own cars.

For a time in the early nineteenth century, the area west of the Cuyahoga River was a separate municipality. Its principal street was Main Street, which extended east across the river on a low swing bridge. For decades, most people in Cleveland were not aware that there was a Main Street in the city. In 1939, $6,000,000 in bonds were issued

47 New Main Avenue Bridge, Cleveland, Ohio

so that motorists had another fine high-level route across the flats in 1941. Traffic was thus lured away from the Public Square on the north side as well as on the south. This bridge connects the Shore Drive on the east with Bulkley Boulevard on the west.

The Largest Concrete Span Bridge in the World,
Rocky River, Ohio.

This 280-foot central span completed in 1910 was claimed to be the "longest concrete span in existence." The bluff overlooking the Rocky River on the eastern side had been the site of taverns from the early days. Later, bowling, dancing, and picnics took place. This point could be reached in the mid-nineteenth century by both steamers on Lake Erie and a "dummy"-type steam railroad. In the twenties, the piers of this bridge next to the concrete structure could still be seen.

C-3—Part of Loading and Runway Area
Cleveland Airport, Cleveland, Ohio

In 1925, when construction of the new Terminal was well under way, the city of Cleveland opened 100 acres of its airport. No airlines were in service to the city at that time. The only traffic consisted of four mail planes that traveled in each direction. To stimulate interest in aviation, Cleveland sponsored the National Air Races each year. Thousands of people came by auto and streetcar to watch the show. The photo for this card was taken in the 1950's when the DC-7B was the pride of Eastern Air Lines.

Bibliography

The basic reference book on the history of Cleveland from its founding to 1950 is *Cleveland, The Making of a City* by William Ganson Rose, published in 1950 by the World Publishing Company of Cleveland. It was produced with the cooperative efforts of scores of people and has chapters devoted to each decade for 154 years from 1796 to 1950. Events are arranged consecutively by year, and the index is quite complete, making it easy to use. I am most indebted to this source for names of individuals and organizations, locations, dates, and relationships.

Other sources used in preparing this publication include:

BOOKS

Applegate, Ray D. *Trolleys and Streetcars on American Picture Post Cards*. New York: Dover Publications, 1979.

Christiansen, Harry. *Northern Ohio's Interurbans and Rapid Transit Railways*. Cleveland: Rapid Transit Data, Inc.

———. *Northern Ohio's Interurbans and Rapid Transit Railways*, revised and enlarged. Euclid OH: Trolley Lore, 1983.

———. *Ohio Trolley Trails*. Vol. 1, *Ohio Series*. Euclid Ohio: Transit House, Inc., 1971.

———. *Trolley Trails*. Vol. 2, *Greater Cleveland and Northern Ohio*. Cleveland: Western Reserve Historical Society, 1975.

———. *Trolley Trails Through Greater Cleveland and Northern Ohio From 1910 to Today*. Vol. 3, *Greater Cleveland and Northern Ohio*. Cleveland: Western Reserve Historical Society. 1975.

———. *New Lake Shore Electric*. Vol. 4, *Greater Cleveland and Northern Ohio*. Cleveland: Western Reserve Historical Society, 1975.

Goulder, Grace. *John D. Rockefeller, The Cleveland Years*. Cleveland: Western Reserve Historical Society, 1975.

Hatcher, Harlan. *Lake Erie*. The American Lake Series. Indianapolis: The Bobbs Merrill Company, 1945.

———. The Western Reserve: *The Story of New Connecticut in Ohio*. Indianapolis: The Bobbs-Merrill Company, 1940.

Izant, Grace Goulder. *This is Ohio: Ohio's 88 Counties in Words and Pictures*. Cleveland: The World Publishing Company, 1953.

Lorenz, Carl. *Tom L. Johnson, Mayor of Cleveland*. New York: The A. S. Barnes Company, 1911.

Morse, Kenneth S. P. *A History of the Cleveland Streetcars from the Time of Electrification*. Baltimore: Kenneth S. P. Morse, 1955.

———. *Ohio Trolleys*. Baltimore: Kenneth S. P. Morse, 1960.

MAPS, PAMPHLETS, PERIODICALS, and OTHER SOURCES

A Chronicle of Cleveland (with comment upon odd diversities throughout the Nation), 1878-1940.

City Visitor 2, No. 7: no date.

Cleveland on Beautiful Lake Erie. Cleveland Convention Board of the Chamber of Commerce, ca. 1920.

Commercial Atlas. 63rd ed. Chicago: Rand, McNally and Company, 1932.

Great Lakes Exposition. Official Souvenir Guide, 1932. Hehr, Russell A. Personal Recollections.

"Map of Cleveland," *Business Atlas*. Chicago: Rand, McNally and Company, 1898: 186.

"Map of Cleveland." Chicago: Rand, McNally and Company, 1893.

"Northern Ohio Live," Cleveland: *M. Magazine, Ltd.*, July 1989.

The Official Guide of the Railways and Steam Navigation Lines of the United States and Canada. New York: National Railway Publication Company. June 1893; June 1916.

Official Street Atlas of Cleveland and Cuyahoga County. Cleveland: Mountcastle Map Company, #7381. No date [ca.1938].

The Union Station. Cleveland: The Cleveland Union Terminals Company, 1930.

"The Yellow Pages," The Cleveland Telephone Directory, 1989.

POSTCARD SUPPLIERS

Batchelder, Marvin. Kew Gardens, New York. A collection acquired from his former teacher and neighbor May Beech of Medina, Ohio.

Bowker, Richard, Pittsburgh, Pa. Personal collection.

Hehr, Russell A. Personal collection acquired by Harvey Roehl of The Vestal Press, Ltd.

Sims, George R. Gainesville, Florida. Formerly of Shaker Heights, Ohio.

Thompson, Paul E. Personal collection and cards inherited from Maud Burnham Thompson (1882-1964).

Thompson, Ralph B. Personal collection plus cards purchased from various dealers, 1989 - 1991.

Index